Holiday Recipes for a
Family Affair

BY Kathy Garver
and Scot Weaver

Foreword by
Christopher Knight

Holiday Recipes for a Family Affair
© 2019. Kathy Garver & Scot Weaver. All rights reserved.

All illustrations are copyright of their respective owners, and are also reproduced here in the spirit of publicity. Whilst we have made every effort to acknowledge specific credits whenever possible, we apologize for any omissions, and will undertake every effort to make any appropriate changes in future editions of this book if necessary.

No part of this book may be reproduced in any form or by any means, electronic, mechanical, digital, photocopying or recording, except for the inclusion in a review, without permission in writing from the publisher.

Published in the USA by:
BearManor Media
P O Box 71426
Albany, Georgia 31708
www.bearmanormedia.com

Printed in the United States of America

ISBN   978-1-62933-412-7 (paperback)
            978-1-62933-413-4 (hardcover)

Book and cover design and layout by Darlene Swanson • www.van-garde.com

Contents

Introduction Kathy Garver and Scot Weaver v

Dedication vii

Foreword ix

Chapter 1   January Scot Weaver. 1

Chapter 2   February Kathy Garver. 25

Chapter 3   March Scot Weaver 49

Chapter 4   April Kathy Garver 59

Chapter 5   May Scot Weaver. 79

Chapter 6   June Kathy Garver. 99

Chapter 7   July Scot Weaver 117

Chapter 8   August Kathy Garver 129

Chapter 9   September Scot Weaver 149

Chapter 10   October Kathy Garver 159

Chapter 11   November Scot Weaver. 187

Chapter 12   December Kathy Garver 201

Index. 235

About the Authors 237

Holidays always make it fun for the family to get together. Uncle Bill (Brian Keith) and Mr. French (Sebastian Cabot) get busy trying to understand the kids at party time Cissy (Kathy Garver), Jody (Johnny Whitaker), and Buffy (Anissa Jones).

Introduction

WHO DOESN'T LOVE A holiday! Oh sure, there's the stress, the traffic, time spent. But then it is all worthwhile - the passing down of traditions, the smile of a job well done. Traditions have always been important in my family - on TV and off. The warmth and remembrances and gathering of favorite friends and family help to make new traditions. Since I love to cook and carry on traditions, I wanted to share my recipes for other people to enjoy. One of my favorite friends, Scot Weaver, had the same idea. Together we created a cookbook to help alleviate that stress, that traffic and, well, maybe not the time spent as some of our recipes call for a dedication to cutting and dicing and oven time, but others - a snap! Enjoy both and enjoy the holidays!

Even Mrs. Beasley enjoys getting her portrait made for the holidays!

Dedications

KATHY GARVER: HOLIDAY RECIPES for A Family Affair is dedicated to my son, Reid Garver Travis, who loves to cook and loves holidays! He taught me to have courage in the kitchen, to try new recipes and new foods. The combination of good meals with exciting new recipes added to my traditional way of cooking and enhanced all our holiday celebrations. Thank you, Reid, for your encouragement, support, and for formulating new traditions in our kitchen.

Scot Weaver: To my parents, Jack and Lauralee Weaver, thank you for giving me a love of cooking. So much of what I learned came from the two of you, from day to day cooking to Holiday cooking. I owe my love for experimentation to my father; he was all about trying new foods. You didn't have to eat it all, just try it! Thanks, Dad.

To my grandmother, Linnie Hand Jacobs Bogen, thank you for passing on your recipes to me. At 97 you are still in the kitchen cooking up delicious meals and I am always amazed, pleased and comforted by your food!

To my boys and their significant others, I wish I had cooked more with you when you were young. Treat your kitchens like a space to be enjoyed and played in with your families. You won't regret it! All my love!

Special thanks to Kathy Garver for her undying friendship and her dedication to bringing this book to life! Thank you for all you do and for who you are!

Foreword by Christopher Knight

HOLIDAY TIME, THE MOST wonderful time of the year! And at the center of all holiday celebrations is food! It makes perfect sense that food and celebrations go together – both are best enjoyed with company. In fact, the Latin root meaning of companion is "with bread" (com = with; pan=bread). So, it's only right that at those times of the year we celebrate a holiday, we do so in the company of family and friends and abundant food.

In the same way, every meal is a small celebration of life. For the chef it's an act of giving; for those eating, an act of reception, and for all a time of gratefulness. In sharing a meal, we share life-sustaining manna. To live we must eat, so let's eat well!

My mother was a wonderful cook. She was self-taught and thoroughly adventurous. There were no picky eaters in my family. I've often wondered if that was because my mother was a good cook, or if it happened because we were all eagerly intrepid eaters. Regardless, if she made it, we ate it. Now, my real family was no Brady bunch. Not close! But there was a perfect harmony in my family in one place, the dinner table.

Like Kathy, I grew up with two families. Having a second, TV family presented an alternate reality and in doing so, an alternate perspective on family. The upside of being a Brady, was we were all expected to be… well, very Brady; kind and considerate to one another. This made for especially supportive and satisfying holidays. The downside was… well, the Brady dinner table – the meals to be specific. Every time we had a dinner scene I couldn't wait to tear into the food. You would have thought I was being starved at home. but every time I'd remember thinking it wasn't like Mom's. It didn't help that our dinner scenes would take four hours to shoot and that they were cooked in the prop room by our prop master, Irving! Like any kid, I suspected life (and dinner) was same for everyone and everyone's mom was a good cook. Doing *The Brady Bunch* taught me not all families were the same, and that not all cooks were good cooks!

When I was finishing high school and after we were done shooting *The Brady Bunch*, I sorely missed the alternate reality of being a Brady. No longer having the Bradys as a functional counterbalance to my own dysfunctional family, I looked forward to becoming an adult, moving out and creating a home and life, *sans* the drama and discord – a more Brady-like life. There was, however, one thing I was going to miss - my mom's cooking!

Nearly an adult, I was now fully aware of how gifted my mom was with food preparation. I was also aware how much good home-cooking had come to mean to me. There was only one thing to do…learn how to cook for myself! At seventeen, my adventures in the kitchen thus began.

I took to cooking like a Beagle on a bone. Learning how to cook was one-part mom's advice and two-parts cookbook. The kitchen is my favorite room in the house – it's my lab and the center of entertainment. It took a number of years to get to the point where I could do Thanksgiving without it doing me but there I was, at twenty-five, cooking Thanksgiving for twenty – family, friends and strays. Soon after it was also Christmas and Easter. With the ability to prepare the holiday meal, I was able to host the holiday. In gaining that ability, I was not only able to repay my mother and father for their years of holiday toil but able to influence the family dynamic so that holiday celebrations were a bit more Brady.

My mother is no longer with us, but I can safely say, while in the kitchen, I channel her.

Kathy and Scot's *Holiday Recipes for a Family Affair* brings a warming nostalgia of family and dining with excellent menus and recipes we can all enjoy!

Happy Celebrating,
Christopher Knight

Actor (*Brady Bunch*), Reality Star (*The Surreal Life, Dancing with the Stars,* and more) Businessman (Christopher Knight Home).

Portrait of Uncle Bill, Mr. French, Buffy, Jody and me, Cissy, sitting for our portrait.

January

JANUARY IS ALL ABOUT New Year's Day and in my house, it was also about College Bowl games, the NFL Playoffs and the Super Bowl. This meant celebrating with our extended neighborhood families. They would gather at our house for great food. My family was a big football family. These bowl games were celebrated as holidays in my family, too. When I grew up and had my own family the celebrations didn't change, what changed was some of the food. Here are my favorites to make and serve whether for New Year's dinner or a football celebration.

New Year's Dinner
(Pork, Beef, Chicken or Fish)

Appetizer
Salami Rolls

First Course
Spicy Mac and Cheese

Entrée
Beer Baked Pork/Prime Rib Roast/
Root Beer Roasted Chicken/Coconut Prawns
Garlic Roasted Red Potatoes
Bacon Wrapped Asparagus

Dessert
Chocolate Raisin Cake

Recipes

Salami Rolls

Ingredients

1   lb. of sliced salami
1   8 oz. package of cream cheese
1   jar of pepperoncini, pickled jalapenos, or pimento stuffed green olives
1   8 oz. can crushed pineapple
1   package of toothpicks

Directions

Open your salami and cream cheese. Drain anything with juice. If you use pineapple, be sure to press and drain the pineapple to be sure all liquid is out.

With a small spoon, scoop about half a spoon of cream cheese to the center of the salami.

Top the cream cheese with the filling(s) you have chosen.

Roll the salami and put a toothpick through the center (the edges of the salami should overlap a bit) to hold the roll closed.

Place them on a serving tray and cover with plastic wrap and place in refrigerator until ready to serve. Only do one day ahead of time.

Spicy Mac and Cheese

Ingredients:

2	cups uncooked macaroni
½	cup mozzarella cheese
½	cup cheddar cheese (I prefer sharp, but use to your taste)
½	cup Monterey Jack cheese
2	small-to-medium fresh jalapeños diced
1	lb. of bacon, cooked and chopped into small pieces
1¼	tsps. salt
1	tsp. butter
	Nonstick spray

Directions:

Put about 6 cups water in a large pot. Add a ¼ tsp. salt and 1 tsp. butter. Bring to boil. Add the 2 cups uncooked macaroni to the boiling water. Bring to boil and simmer until macaroni is not quite finished cooking. It will finish during baking. Drain and dry the macaroni. In a large bowl, place the noodles, all the cheese (except hold back about ¼ cup of all the cheese for topping near the end), add the jalapeños, bacon and teaspoon of salt. Mix thoroughly and set aside. Take a 9x13-inch pan and spray with nonstick spray. Add the mac and cheese mixture and cover with foil. Preheat the oven to 375 degrees. Once the oven is at temperature, place the mac and cheese in the center of the center rack. Cook for 40 minutes or until bubbling. Remove the pan and the foil. Turn oven up to 425 degrees. Use the ¼ cup of cheese to sprinkle on top of the mac and cheese. Place back in the oven for 10 minutes or until cheese on top is golden brown. Remove from oven and let stand for 10 minutes before serving.

Beer Baked Boneless Pork Chops

Ingredients

    One boneless pork chop for each person
1   can or bottle of beer, your choice
    Salt
    Pepper
    Garlic powder
3   tablespoons olive oil
    Fresh rosemary

Directions

Preheat the oven to 375. Put three tablespoons of olive oil in a skillet. Salt, pepper and add a little garlic powder to each chop. Sear each chop in the olive oil and place in baking pan or leave in iron skillet. Once all chops are in the pan, place four sprigs of fresh rosemary around the chops and pour the beer over the chops. Place the pan of chops in the oven and bake for 35 minutes. Make sure the internal temperature reaches 145 degrees. Let rest for about 5 minutes and plate. Strain the juices into a bowl and guest can use if they like.

Prime Rib Roast

About the Cut: People like this cut with bone left intact and others prefer to have the bone removed. The meat is much tastier if cooked with the bone. I recommend that you ask your butcher to cut the rib off, but tie it back together for cooking.

Ingredients

    Rib roast (size for number of people you are feeding)
2   pounds of rock salt
    Crushed pepper

Directions

Preheat the oven to 325 degrees. Get a roasting pan big enough for the rib roast. Fill half the pan with rock salt. Put crushed pepper over the outside of the rib roast (meat side). Place that side down into the rock salt. Cover with foil (or lid to pan if it has one). Place in the preheated oven and cook for 15 minutes for each pound. About an hour before cook time is done, remove foil and continue cooking. About 20 minutes before the cook time is done, insert thermometer to check internal temperature. The internal temperature should be at a minimum of 145 degrees. When it reaches that temperature, remove the roast and allow it to rest for at least 10 minutes before cutting and serving. *

*Note: Cooking this way will leave you no juices to create any *au jus*. But the flavor of the meat stands alone.

To cook without rock salt, place the peppered rib roast on rack in baking pan rib down. Cooking instructions for time and temperature are the same. When finished you can strain the *au jus* and place in a bowl and serve for spooning onto roast.

Root Beer Roasted Chicken

Ingredients:

4	thighs
4	breasts
2	cans of root beer
	Salt
	Pepper

Directions:
Preheat the oven to 350 degrees. Pour one can of root beer in a bowl. Place the chicken in that bowl. Add water to cover the chicken and leave in refrigerator for at least 1 hour and no longer than overnight. Use a roasting pan and spray it with nonstick spray. Place the chicken in the pan. Salt and pepper both sides of the chicken. Pour the other can of root beer over the chicken and cover. Cook for about 35 minutes. Uncover the chicken and cook for another 15 minutes. Check the internal temperature and remove from oven if it has reached 165 degrees. If it has not, continue to check every 5 minutes or so until it has reached the 165 degrees. Let the chicken rest for about 10 minutes before serving. You can use the drippings to make chicken gravy.

Coconut Prawns

Ingredients:

24	large prawns
1	small bag of shredded coconut
	Salt
	Pepper
2	sticks of butter

Directions:

Clean, rinse and dry the prawns. Fill a small bowl with shredded coconut. Melt one stick of butter in a bowl. Dip your prawns in the butter, and roll that in the coconut and set on a piece of parchment paper. In a cast-iron skillet (or any frying pan you have), melt the other stick of butter on medium heat. Place the prawns in the pan once the butter is melted and cook on both sides until the prawns' flesh is a nice pink color, about 4 minutes.

Garlic Roasted Red Potatoes

Ingredients:

6	medium red potatoes washed and cut in half
⅓	cup of olive oil
	Garlic powder
	Salt
	Pepper

Directions:

Preheat the oven to 375 degrees. Place the washed and cut potatoes in a large mixing bowl. Pour the ⅓ cup of olive oil over the potatoes and mix. Make sure the potatoes are covered in olive oil (you can add more as needed). Place the potatoes on a cookie sheet (only one layer). Then sprinkle garlic powder, salt and pepper over them. Place on the middle rack and bake at 375 degrees for 45 minutes or until a nice golden-brown top and a fork can be poked into the potato and the potato falls off the fork.

Bacon Pecan Asparagus

Ingredients

2	pounds asparagus (adjust according to number of guests)
1	pound of bacon
¼	cup of extra virgin olive oil
⅓	cup of brown sugar
¼	cup of pecans
1	pinch of salt

Directions:

Wash and dry the asparagus. Cut the bottom edges of the asparagus off and disregard those pieces. Place the asparagus into a bowl. Drizzle olive oil over the asparagus and with tongs toss until asparagus is covered in olive oil. Lay out all asparagus on paper towel and add a pinch of salt over the top of them. Place parchment paper in a cookie sheet. Wrap asparagus in a piece of bacon and place on cookie sheet. Repeat until all are wrapped. Set aside for a moment. Turn your oven on to 375 degrees. In a small bowl, mix your brown sugar and pecans until the pecans are coated. Take this pecan mixture and sprinkle over the asparagus. Place in 375-degree oven and cook for 20 minutes. Check at the 15-minute mark to be sure the bacon and asparagus are not over cooking. Remove from oven and let them sit for 5 minutes and then place on serving tray.*

*Note: You may serve hot or cold. If you want them cold, you will cover them with plastic wrap (after they cool) and place them in refrigerator until you are ready to serve.

Rich Chocolate Applesauce Cake

Ingredients

2	cups all-purpose flour
2	cups sugar
¾	cup of powder cocoa
2	tsps. baking powder
1½	tsps. baking soda
1	tsp. salt
1	tsp. espresso powder
1	cup of raisins (can be excluded if you dislike them)
1	cup of walnuts (can be excluded if allergies or dislike them)
1	cup of whole milk
½	cup unsweetened applesauce
2	eggs
2	tsps. vanilla extract
1	cup boiling water

*Note: frosting recipe to follow

Directions:

Sift together in a large mixing bowl or free-standing mixer flour, cocoa powder, baking powder, baking soda, and salt and espresso powder. Add sugar, raisins, walnuts and whisk together. Add milk, applesauce, eggs and vanilla extract and mix together on medium speed until well combined. Reduce the speed and carefully add the boiling water to the batter. Beat on high speed for about 1 minute to add air to the batter. Your batter is going to look very thin, this is ok and how it is supposed to look. Set it aside and grease and flour two 9-inch round or 1 9x13-inch pan. Pour batter into cake pan(s) evenly. Place in a 350-degree oven on the middle rack and bake for 30-35 minutes, until toothpick or cake tester inserted in the center comes out clean. Remove from oven and cool. Once cooled enough to remove from pan and placed on rack, do that and allow it to finish cooling. While cooling, make the frosting. Recipe is below.

Vanilla Frosting

Ingredients:

½ cup of cold whole milk or heavy cream

3 cups confectioners' sugar

1 tsp. vanilla extract

Directions:

Add all ingredients to a mixing bowl and use the whisk attachment and whip on high until all ingredients are combined to a rich, smooth frosting look. Add more liquid if too dry, add more sugar if too wet. If the cake is cool enough to frost without melting the frosting, frost the cake and it is ready to serve. If cake is still too warm to frost, cover the frosting and set it aside until cake is ready.

January

Getting ready for the rain, Buffy, Jody and Cissy envision what great meals for the holidays they are going to help Mr. French make - much to his chagrin sometimes!

Bowl Game

Appetizer
Nacho Bar

First Course
Little BBQ Bear Sausages

Entrée
Beef, Chicken, Pork and Fish Tacos
Pico de Gallo

Dessert
Chewy Chocolate Oatmeal Cookies

Recipes

Easy Nacho

Ingredients:

1	lb. of lean ground beef, steak, chicken breast, or shredded pork
1	tbsp. oil
1	lb. sharp cheddar cheese
½	cup sour cream
1	12 oz. bottle of beer
1	head of lettuce
3	beefsteak tomatoes
1	large sweet onion
3	large avocados
1	lime
1	or 2 bags of tortilla chips*
	Salt
	Pepper
	Mexican seasoning (or a package of taco seasoning)
16	oz. of refried beans

Directions:

You can cut up all the following and place in containers a day ahead or earlier in the same day and keep in refrigerator until ready to serve. Grate the cheese and set aside. Rinse and dry the lettuce. Chop lettuce finely. Dice all three tomatoes and place into container. Dice onion and place into container. Right before you are ready to serve, you will dice your avocado and take the other half of the lime and squeeze the juice over the diced avocado and with a potato masher, mash the avocado until smooth. Add pinch of salt and sour cream to the avocado and mix well. Cover and refrigerate until ready to serve. The meat needs to be fully cooked. If you use the shredded pork it is the only one that needs to be cooked ahead of time. The steak, once cooked, needs to be sliced into small strips (easy for chewing). Place the meat you have chosen into a pan with 1 tablespoon of oil. Cook the meat or heat it up if already cooked thoroughly. Once cooked, drain all fat off. Add pinch of salt and pepper, add in package of taco seasoning (or 1 tablespoon of Mexican seasoning) and ¼ cup of water. Cook until liquid is absorbed. Place in crock pot to keep hot. Take your grated cheese and ¼ cup of heavy cream and place in saucepan on medium heat. Stir constantly. Once the cheese and cream are melted and blended add the bottle of room-temperature beer. Continue to cook on medium heat until it is blended well. Transfer to crock pot for keeping hot and serving.

Place the tortillas in foil, heat tortillas in an oven at 300 degrees with a pan of water on the rack below. Serve tortillas in the foil wrap to keep warm.

If you used canned beans, place them in a crock pot on low and heat them up for serving. You will need to stir occasionally.

*Note: Below are recipes for making your own refried beans and tortilla

Recipe for your own refried beans

Ingredients:

2	8-ounce bags of pinto beans
¼	quarter cup of lard
2	teaspoons of salt

Directions:

Rinse the pinto beans. Place the beans in a pot and cover beans with cold water and pinch of salt. Let them soak at least 3 hours. Drain the beans and place back in pot with cold water. Cover the beans and be sure you have about 1 to 1½ inches of water above the beans. Add another pinch of salt. Place on stove at high heat until it boils. Once it boils lower heat to simmer. Stir occasionally. The time here will differ for many reasons. But watch it, and let it cook down until the beans have thickened. Cook the beans until they will mash with a fork easily. Drain the excess water off. Put the beans back in the pot and with a potato masher mash the beans until they look like what a can of refried beans looks like. Place them on low heat add the ¼ cup of lard and 2 teaspoons of salt. Continue to stir until the lard is melted and blended in. Transfer this to a crock pot to keep hot (low setting is fine).

Home Made Tortilla Chips

Ingredients:
1   bag of soft taco tortillas
    Salt
    Oil for pan or deep fryer

Directions:
Cut all the soft taco tortillas into triangles. Add oil to a pan so that if you place the tortilla triangles into the oil it will cover them. Or use the deep fryer. The oil temperature should be at 325 degrees. Place tortillas in oil and cook to golden brown (you have to eye this, they are easy to burn). Once cooked, remove them from the oil and place on paper towels to allow excess oil to drip away. Immediately add salt to taste. Place in serving dish.

Little BBQ Sausages

Ingredients:

1	package of bite-sized sausages
1	bottle of beer
1	bottle of BBQ sauce
½	cup of grape jelly

Directions:

Put the BBQ sauce, beer, and grape jelly into a crock pot. Mix that thoroughly. Now add the package of sausage to it. Cook on low all day until ready to serve. Be sure it has cooked for at least 4 hours. Serve from crock pot with toothpicks.

Beef, Chicken, Pork and Fish Tacos

Ingredients:

1	lb. ground round
4	chicken thighs
½	pound of pork shoulder
½	pound of halibut
	Salt
	Pepper
	Cumin
	Garlic powder
	Vegetable oil
1	quart of vegetable stock
	Enough corn tortillas for your guests

Directions:

In a frying pan, brown the ground beef. Add 1 tsp. salt, 1 tsp. pepper, 1 tsp. cumin, and 1 tsp. garlic powder. Stir into the meat and let the meat cook thoroughly. Set aside until you are ready to serve.

Place 2 tbsps. of vegetable oil in a pan. Place the four chicken thighs in that pan. Add 1 tsp. of salt, 1 tsp. of pepper, 1 tsp. of cumin, and 1 tsp. of garlic powder. Cook chicken until done. Cut the chicken into small cubes and set aside until ready to serve.

Pour the vegetable stock into a saucepan. Add 1 tsp. salt, 1 tsp. pepper, 1 tsp. cumin, and 1 tsp. garlic powder into the vegetable broth. Rinse the pork shoulder and rub in about 2 tsps. of salt. Let that sit for about two minutes. After the pork has sat for two minutes, place it into the vegetable broth. Bring this to a roaring boil and turn the heat down to let it simmer for about 2 hours. Keep checking the pork to be sure the liquid does not boil out. After the two hours, remove pork from the heat. Remove the pork shoulder from the saucepan and let it rest for ten minutes. After the pork has rested, cut it into cubes and set aside until ready to serve.

Place 2 tbsp. of vegetable oil in a saucepan. Cut the fish into cubes. Season the fish with 1 tsp. salt, 1 tsp. pepper, 1 tsp. cumin, and 1 tsp. garlic powder. Place the saucepan on burner that is turned to high. Once the oil in the pan is hot, place the seasoned fish into the pan. Sear the fish on both sides (this should take about one minute and thirty seconds each side). Remove the fish and set aside until you are ready to serve.

Right before you are ready to serve, place all the meat into the oven (temperature should be at 225 degrees) to warm all the meat.

While you are warming the meat, you will warm the tortillas. Use a nonstick pan and place it over medium heat. Place a tortilla in the pan and warm it for about 30 seconds each side. Place into a container that allows the food to retain its heat. Set aside until ready to serve.

Pico de Gallo

Ingredients:

- 3 beef steak tomatoes
- 3 garlic cloves
- 2 jalapeños
- 1 medium onion
- 1 bunch of cilantro
- 1 tsp. salt
- 1 tsp. pepper

Directions:

Dice the tomatoes and place in a mixing bowl. Mince the garlic and place in the bowl with the tomatoes. Remove the tops and seeds of the jalapeños. Dice the jalapeños and place with the other ingredients. Dice the onion finely and place with the other ingredients. Cut the stems off the cilantro and discard. Chop what is left of the cilantro finely and add to rest of ingredients. Mix this well. Add the salt and pepper to the mixture. Mix well again, cover, and refrigerate until you are ready to serve.

Chewy Chocolate Oatmeal Cookies

Ingredients:

¾	cup of all-purpose flour
½	cup oats
½	cup chocolate chips
¼	cup cocoa powder
½	tsp. baking soda
¼	tsp. salt
¾	cup butter softened
½	cup sugar
½	cup firmly packed brown sugar
1	egg
1	tsp. vanilla extract

Direction

In a large bowl, sift flour, cocoa powder, baking soda and salt. Add the oats to the bowl and whisk together. Set this bowl aside. In a mixing bowl, beat the butter until fluffy. Add the sugar and beat again until creamy. Add the egg and vanilla and beat until creamy. Add the flour mixture a ⅓ at a time and mix well before adding the next ⅓, until all is mixed well. Add the chocolate chips and mix well again. Refrigerate for 1 hour. Place parchment paper on cookie sheets. Preheat the oven to 350 degrees. Get your cookie dough from refrigerator and a cookie scoop. Place cookies 2 inches apart. Place on middle rack and back for 12-15 minutes or until cookie is slightly firm in middle and cracked on top. Remove and place on cooling rack. Can be served warm or cooled.

We all enjoy a holiday party and birthday - even if Mr French gets the same present!

February

WHAT DOES FEBRUARY BRING? It brings romance, a desire for comfort from the cold, and the opportunity to create tasty thoughtful dishes for your family. Whether you are an empty nester, a family with children and/or teens or just a couple in love, the following menus and recipes are sure to bring you closer together. In my personal situation, at this writing, I have a 27-year-old son, Reid, who lives in the "basement" of our family home with his 27-year- old fiancée. For Valentine's Day my husband and I trade with the young couple to see who is going to dine at home and which duo is going out. My son is a wonderful and creative cook and in 2018 the decision was made he was going to stay in. I'll share some of the recipes he cooked to wow his intended and the one I made when it was my husband's and my turn to stay in! Reid went with the meat selection, this was before he turned vegetarian, but following are menus with easy-to-make dishes whether you are creating wonderful meals for your extended family, the two of you or making a luscious single meal with . . . chocolate truffles for dessert!

Valentine Meat Entrée for Two

Appetizer
Figs Stuffed with Cheese

First Course
Chilled Shrimp situated to look
over a delicious tangy cocktail or
remoulade sauce below in a
sparkling glass bowl

Entrée
Beef Wellington with Red Wine Sauce
Petite Potatoes sautéed in Garlic Olive Oil and Creamy Butter
Asparagus with Hollandaise Sauce

Dessert
Cherries Jubilee
Paired with what wine?
A nice cabernet . . . or champagne is always
good for a romantic interlude!
Try a rose champagne to complete the theme.

Valentine's poultry recipe for the family

Appetizer

A collection of favorite nuts, including macadamia and cashews, peanuts for the kids (if they don't have an allergy to them). Have the young ones pour them into some small dishes around the house — keep the nuts away from the dogs!

First Course

Tomato Bisque Soup with Heart-Shaped Croutons

Entrée

Cornish Game Hens with Orange Glaze

Wild and Brown Rice

Broccoli in Lemon Butter Sauce

Dessert

Cherry Ice Cream with Heart-Shaped Cookies

Drinks: Sparkling water with fresh strawberries and mint garnish

Valentine Fish Menu

Appetizer
Brie with Champignon and Heart-Shaped Lahvosh Crackers.
Seedless Red Grapes.

First Course
Baby lettuces with glazed walnuts and cranberries,
blue cheese, tossed with a champagne vinaigrette

Entrée
Salmon En Papillote
Broccoli with Lemon Butter Sauce
Mashed Potatoes with Truffle Butter

Dessert
Chocolate Molten Lava Cake
Dessert includes lots of love!
Chilled Chardonnay from Napa Valley or Champagne

Recipes

Figs Stuffed with Cheese

Ingredients:

- 6 fresh figs
- 3 oz. goat cheese (herbed chèvre)
- 6 slices prosciutto
- Square of honeycomb
- Sliced French bread

Directions:

Preheat oven to 400 degrees. Trim about ½-inch off the top of each fig. Make a cross about ¾ inches down on each one. Gently press open and put ½ oz. of cheese into the center. Surround the fig with a slice of prosciutto. Sit the fig on a greased or a parchment-lined baking sheet. If the figs are a little wobbly, take a little off the bottom so they may sit up straight. Cook the stuffed figs for 15-20 minutes or until the prosciutto is crispy.

Place on a decorative tray with the honeycomb and sliced bread.

You might want to serve some champagne or wine to start your special Valentine's dinner!

Beef Wellington

Ingredients:

2	4-5 oz. beef tenderloin or filet mignon
1	clove garlic cut in half
	Sea salt and ground pepper
2	tbsps. butter
2	tbsps. brandy
¼	cup fresh mushrooms, minced
2	tbsps. shallots, minced
1	2 oz. can pork or duck liver pâté
	Flat leaf parsley for garnish

Sauce:

2	tbsps. shallots minced
3	large mushrooms, sliced
2	tbsps. white flour
¼	cup red wine, table or burgundy
1	cup beef broth
1	tbsp. fresh thyme, snipped

Pastry:

3	Pepperidge Farm puff pastry sheets, thawed, cut in 7-inch squares - follow directions on the package to prepare the sheets. Roll out the sheets to approx. ¼ inches.
2	eggs, beaten, for wash
	Butter

Directions:
Rub the filet with the garlic halves and then sprinkle with the salt and pepper. Melt butter and sauté filets in pan for 2-3 minutes on each side. Remove from heat. Warm and then flame the brandy - away from the stove and pour over the filets. Loosely cover the filets and refrigerate.

In the same pan, sauté the chopped mushrooms for the duxelle. Remove from pan and refrigerate to chill. When chilled, mix with pâté. Spread mixture over the filets and return to the refrigerator.

For the pastry:
Roll out the defrosted sheets on a lightly floured surface and cut them into two seven-inch squares. Brush with beaten egg and place chilled filets in each of the squares, pâté side down. Bring the ends and the sides of the sheets up to meet like a package and pinch together. Seal with butter or more beaten egg. Turn over the wrapped fillet and cut four small slits in the tops of the pastry.

Place the filets on a greased baking pan sealed side down and brush again with the beaten egg. I cut out hearts and flowers from the remaining dough and put them on top of each filet and then brush them again with egg.

Bake at 400 degrees for 25-30 minutes until the meat is done to your likeness (I like mine medium) and the pastry is golden brown.

Meanwhile, for the sauce, in the same pan as the mushrooms, sauté shallots and sliced mushrooms in butter for about 3-5 minutes or until tender. Combine flour and broth until smooth then stir into the mushroom mixture. Bring to a boil and cook and stir until thickened (about 2 minutes). Stir in wine and thyme. Cook and stir about 2 minutes longer. Add salt and pepper and remove from heat. Serve with beef and garnish with flat-leafed parsley.

Petite Potatoes with Garlic
(as long as you're both having garlic ...)

Ingredients:

½	bag of tiny, one bite, tri-colored potatoes
	Extra virgin or garlic olive oil
2-4	cloves of garlic, minced
2	tbsps. butter
1	tbsp. chopped fresh parsley
½	tsp. sea salt
½	tsp. white pepper
½	tbsp. fresh snipped dill

Directions

Wash potatoes. Cover with water in a small saucepan. Bring to a boil and simmer for about 10 minutes or until tender. Do not overcook. Drain.

Meanwhile, over medium heat, add enough oil to cover bottom of a skillet. When fragrant, melt butter and stir together with olive oil. Add garlic and salt and stir until garlic is tender - about 2-3 minutes. Add parsley, white pepper and dill. Add drained potatoes and coat with butter and garlic mixture.

Asparagus with Hollandaise

Ingredients:

- ½ lb. asparagus
- 2 egg yolks
- ¼ fresh lemon, juiced
- Pinch salt
- ¼ cup butter, melted

Directions:

Wash the asparagus, break off the tough ends. Steam in a rack over boiling water in a steamer or in a shallow pan with about a half-inch of boiling water. When water is boiling, place asparagus in rack, cover and steam for 3-5 minutes or until tender, depending on the breadth of the stalk.

Meantime, make the sauce. Melt the butter. Beat together the egg yolks, lemon juice, and salt in a microwave-safe bowl until smooth. Slowly whisk the ingredients together with the melted butter until incorporated. Heat in microwave 15-20 seconds on high. Whisk again.

Remove the asparagus from the steamer. Place on plate and drizzle hollandaise over the greens.

Cherries Jubilee

Ingredients:

¼	cup butter, cut into chunks
⅓	cup sugar
1	tbsp. cornstarch
1	can dark sweet cherries (15 oz.), drained reserving ¼ cup of juice
1	cinnamon stick broken or cut into two pieces
½	tsp. vanilla
¼	cup or kirsch or cognac, warmed
1	pint vanilla bean ice cream

Directions:

Mix a little cherry juice with cornstarch in small bowl and set aside. Melt butter over medium high heat in 10-inch skillet. Stir in sugar, stirring constantly about 2 minutes. Add rest of cherry juice and cinnamon sticks. Add cornstarch mixture. Continue cooking, stirring occasionally 1-2 minutes until mixture is thickened.

Add cherries and vanilla. Warm. Pour in warmed kirsch or cognac. Flame the pan. Remove cherries from heat.

Scoop ice cream into dessert dishes and spoon warm cherries and sauce over the ice cream. Enjoy!

Tomato Bisque Soup

Ingredients:

3	tbsps. olive oil
2	garlic cloves, minced
1	small onion, sliced
2	carrots peeled and diced
2	cans peeled Roma tomatoes
2	cups of chicken stock
1	tbsp. sugar
½	tbsp. dried basil
1	cup heavy cream
	Salt and white pepper to taste
2	slices sturdy white bread
1½	tbsps. butter

Directions:

Cut 4 heart shapes with cookie cutter from bread. Melt butter in small skillet. Toast croutons on both sides in pan. They may be placed in covered jar or plastic carton until ready for use.

Heat olive oil in a large heavy-bottomed saucepan over medium high heat. Add garlic and sauté for about 30 seconds. Add onions and carrots and cook about ten minutes then add basil and cook 5 minutes more until vegetables are totally soft.

Add tomatoes, broth and sugar. Bring to a boil and then reduce heat to simmer and cook 20-40 minutes. Cool slightly and then purée in food processor or blender.

Return to pot over low heat and stir in cream little by little until soup is just heated through and warmed. Season to taste with salt and pepper, and top with heart-shaped croutons for serving.

Cornish Game Hen with Orange Glaze

Ingredients:

1	1½-1¾ lb. Cornish game hen, halved with backbone removed
1	orange, cut into ½-inch rounds
1	medium onion, cut into ½-inch rounds
1	tbsp. extra virgin olive oil
1	tbsp. water
	Salt and ground black pepper
⅓	cup orange marmalade
1	tbsp. orange juice
1	tbsp. bourbon
1	tsp. fresh ginger, minced
½	tsp. dried tarragon
	Salt and white ground pepper

Directions:

Preheat oven to 450 degrees. Spray a small roasting pan or rimmed baking sheet with cooking oil. Wash and dry cut-halves of Cornish hen. Season with salt and pepper. Arrange orange and onion slices in pan in preparation to top with hen halves. Place them on top of the slices. Rub halves with oil. Bake for fifteen minutes.

Meanwhile, for the glaze, in a heavy small saucepan, combine marmalade, orange juice, bourbon, ginger, tarragon. Simmer over medium heat until thickened, about 4 minutes. Season with salt and pepper.

When the hen has baked for fifteen minutes, brush the halves with marmalade glaze and roast ten minutes longer or until they are a golden brown and the juices run clear basting a couple times during the process.

Transfer the hens to a serving platter and keep warm. Remove all but one orange slice from the baking pan (which can be used to sop up any browned bits) and place on the stove over medium high heat. Add water and simmer. Pour the sauce into a sauce boat and drizzle over warm hens to serve.

Wild and Brown Rice

Ingredients:

1	tsp. extra virgin olive oil
1	shallot minced
1½	cups vegetable broth
½	cup long grain brown rice
¼	cup brown rice
¼	tsp. ground thyme
	Pinch of dried marjoram
	Salt and pepper to taste

Directions:

Briefly heat the oil in a saucepan with a tight-fitting lid. Add the shallot and sauté over medium heat about five minutes, until soft. Add the stock and bring to a boil. Then add the brown and wild rices, thyme, marjoram, salt and pepper. Bring to a boil again and then reduce the heat to low. Cover and simmer for 40 minutes or until rice is tender and liquid is absorbed.

Broccoli with Lemon Butter

Ingredients:

½	lb. broccoli florets
1½	tbsps. butter
1	tbsp. lemon
1	tsp. lemon zest
	Salt and pepper

Directions:

Steam the broccoli until crisp tender, about three minutes. Meanwhile, melt the butter in a skillet. Add the lemon juice and cook for 30 seconds. Stir in the lemon zest, salt and pepper, and then add in the broccoli. Toss to coat.

Sugar Cookies

Ingredients:

3	cups all-purpose flour
2	tsps. baking powder
½	tsp. salt
1	cup granulated sugar
1	cup unsalted butter, room temperature
1	large egg
1	tsp. vanilla extract
	Flour for rolling

For the Icing

1	cup powdered (confectioner's) sugar
2	tsps. milk
2	tsps. light corn syrup
¼	tsp. vanilla extract
	Food coloring

Directions:

Preheat the oven to 350 degrees. Mix together dry ingredients: flour, baking powder and salt, in a large bowl. In the bowl of your mixer, cream the butter and add the sugar mixing until smooth, about three minutes. Beat in eggs and vanilla. Slowly combine the dry ingredients and mix. Remove from bowl and place on a floured surface. With wet hands knead slightly (do not overwork). Roll out the dough with a floured rolling pin to ¼ inches. Dip heart-shaped cookie cutters in flour and cut out shapes.

Bake on a parchment-covered cookie sheet for about seven minutes or until barely golden around the edges. Remove from oven and let sit for five minutes. Put the cookies on a rack to cool completely before icing.

Icing

Stir together the powdered sugar, milk and vanilla in a small bowl. You can make colored icing by putting a little of the frosting in a small bowl and adding red for a bright hue and lesser amounts of red for pink. Purple can be made by adding together red and blue. Put frosting in a plastic bag with a small corner cut off and pipe the cookie with different designs. Fill in rest of icing or just paint the cookies with a small brush or butter knife.

Baby Lettuces with Champagne Vinaigrette

Ingredients:
For the Dressing

2	tbsps. champagne vinaigrette
1½	tsps. Dijon mustard
3	tbsps. extra virgin olive oil

Salad

2	cups of mixed baby greens, washed and dried
1	ripe red Anjou pear, sliced
½	cup crumbled blue cheese
½	bag of dried cranberries and glazed walnut combination

Directions

Whisk together the mustard and vinaigrette in a small bowl. Gradually add the oil continuing to whisk until smooth. Set aside.

Divide and place the lettuces in two serving bowls or plates and top with sliced pears, blue cheese and glazed walnut/cranberry combination. Drizzle dressing evenly over the salad and enjoy!

Kathy and Scot with Baby lettuce Salad that Kathy made for a shoot.

Salmon En Papillote with Dill Sauce

Ingredients

2   six-ounce salmon filets, skin on
1   large shallot, peeled and sliced
1   lemon, one half thinly sliced, other half juiced
1   large zucchini, sliced
    Fresh dill, coarsely chopped
    Extra virgin olive oil
    Salt and white pepper
    Two sheets parchment paper

Directions:

Preheat the oven to 375 degrees. Pat the salmon filets dry and season with salt and pepper. Place the parchment paper side by side on your counter. Divide ½ lemon wheels, shallots and zucchini and put into the center of the parchment sheets. Salt and pepper and drizzle with a little olive oil. Place salmon filets on top of the vegetable mixture. Top with remaining lemon wheels. Drizzle a little oil on top. Bring the sides of the parchment paper together and crimp several times with your fingers until the sides are tightly sealed. Do the same with the ends of the paper. Place the parchment packets on a baking sheet, sealed sides up and cook until the parchment is puffed, about 18-20 minutes.

While the fish is cooking make the lemon dill sauce. In a small bowl, whisk the dill and lemon juice with 1-2 tbsps. of olive oil. Season the fish with salt and pepper.

When salmon can be easily pierced with a skewer, remove from oven. Place the packages on individual plates and carefully open them. Pour the lemon dill sauce over the salmon and serve with truffle potatoes.

Truffle Mashed Potatoes

Ingredients:

1¼	lbs. large Yukon Gold potatoes, peeled and cut into 2-inch chunks
	Salt
	White pepper
¾	cups warm half-and-half
3	tbsps. unsalted butter, at room temperature
3	tbsps. truffle butter, room temperature

Directions:

Place potatoes in large deep saucepan and cover with cold water. Bring to a boil.

Salt the water and turn down the heat to medium heat and cook the potatoes until tender, about twenty minutes.

Drain the potatoes in a colander and return to pan. Turn the heat to medium high and shake the pot until the potatoes are dry, about a minute. Remove from heat.

Mash the potatoes in the pot with a potato masher. Add unsalted butter and one half of the warmed half-and-half. Season with salt and pepper. Continue mashing until the potatoes are creamy. Add the remaining half-and-half and the truffle butter and continue to mash until all is incorporated and smooth. Season with salt and pepper again. To keep the potatoes hot or to reheat them, place them in a heatproof bowl over simmering water in a pot. Heat slowly, adding a little more truffle butter and half-and-half if the potatoes get too thick. Serve hot.

Chocolate Molten Lava Cake

Ingredients:

4	ounces semi-sweet baking chocolate or chocolate chips
½	cup butter
1	cup powdered sugar
2	eggs
2	egg yolks
6	tbsps. flour
	Powdered sugar for dusting the top of cake
16	raspberries, washed and dried

Directions:

Preheat the oven to 425 degrees. Spray four custard cups or small ramekin dishes (6-8 oz.) with cooking spray. Place on a baking sheet and set aside.

Microwave chocolate and butter together in medium microwave bowl on high one minute or until butter is melted. Whisk chocolate and butter until combined and smooth.

Add powdered sugar and stir in evenly. Add whole eggs and egg yolks and beat until well incorporated. Carefully stir in flour and mix well. Spoon mixture into prepared cups (an ice cream scoop is a good aid in this process). Distribute batter evenly into cups.

Place cups on baking sheet and then into preheated oven and bake for 12-13 minutes or until edges are firm but centers are still soft. Let cool for 2 minutes. Run a knife around the cakes to loosen carefully and then invert onto small serving plates. Dust powdered sugar on top of the cakes and place 4 raspberries around each on its dish and enjoy the spectacular Valentine's Day dessert!

Buffy, Jody and Cissy sitting still before we go out to celebrate.

March

MARCH IS THE BEGINNING of spring and St. Patrick's Day celebrations. Growing up, we always had fun around holidays. My parents always made sure that it was about the kids. However, we did not do anything for St. Patrick's Day when I was a child other than wearing green. Once I got to college, I began to celebrate St. Patrick's Day. Many people enjoy a good corned beef and cabbage meal on this day. I too enjoy this meal! However, my favorite is a nice beef stew. Whatever you do to celebrate, enjoy those around you and find as many ways as you can to make the day special and fun!

St. Patrick's Day
(Beef, Pork, Chicken or Fish)

Appetizer
Stuffed Jalapeños

First Course
Bacon, Sesame, Brussels Sprouts

Entrée
Beef/Pork/Chicken Stew/Irish Seafood Stew
Spinach Mashed Potatoes
Cheddar/Monterey Cheese Butter Milk Biscuits

Dessert
Chocolate Peanut Butter Cups

Recipes

Stuffed Jalapeños

Ingredients:

- 6   fresh jalapeños (or as many as you need, 1 per person)
- 1   8 oz. package of cream cheese
- 3   tbsps. extra virgin olive oil

Directions:

Preheat your oven to 400 degrees. I suggest you wear gloves while preparing this dish to avoiding getting the pepper on your hands and accidentally touching other parts of your body. Carefully cut the tops off each pepper. With a small paring knife, remove the seeds and as much of the white membrane as possible without damaging the pepper itself. Once all are done, use a teaspoon and fill each pepper with cream cheese. Set them aside. Cover a cookie sheet with parchment paper. Place the peppers on the parchment paper and brush them with olive oil. Be sure that each pepper was stuffed full, no air at the bottom. Place the peppers on the middle rack and bake for 12 minutes and then rotate the pan and bake for another 12 minutes. The cream cheese should be browned on top and the peppers should look roasted (a few black spots). If not, cook at 5-minute intervals.

Bacon, Sesame, Brussels Sprouts

Ingredients

½	pound of Brussels sprouts
5	pieces of bacon
	Two tsps. sesame seeds
¼	cup olive oil
½	cup balsamic vinegar

Directions

Cut the ends off the Brussels sprouts and then cut them in half. Put ½ cup of balsamic vinegar in a bowl. Add the Brussels sprouts to the vinegar and let soak for about 30 minutes. Put ½ cup of olive oil in a frying pan and place on medium heat. Drain the Brussels sprouts, but keep the vinegar for later. Put the Brussels sprouts in the pan and sauté until the Brussels sprouts begin to caramelize. Now add back about two or three tablespoons of the vinegar and let simmer for about 2 or 3 minutes. Drain and place in serving dish. Sprinkle the sesame seeds over the Brussels sprouts and serve.*

*Note: Brussels sprouts can be served hot or cold.

Hearty Beef Stew (Pork or Chicken)

Ingredients

1	pound of stew meat (1 pound of pork roast diced or ½ of chicken breast diced and ½ of chicken thighs diced)
1	cup of flour
6	red potatoes
1	large onion
5	carrots
4	celery stalks
1	64 oz. container of beef broth
3	tsps. cornstarch
2	tsps. salt
1	tsp. pepper
3	tsps. olive oil

Directions:

Pour one cup of beef broth (use chicken broth with the chicken and vegetable broth with the pork) in a saucepan; pour the remaining broth into the crock pot. Heat the broth on medium heat. Add the three tbsps. of cornstarch, stirring until dissolved. Remove from heat and add to crock pot, stirring it in until well blended. Add one tsp. salt. Whisk flour, 1 tsp. salt and pepper. Dredge the beef, pork or chicken in the flour mixture. Place a frying pan on the stove and put on medium high heat. Add the olive oil and then brown the stew meat on all sides. Add this to the crock pot. Wash and dry 6 red potatoes. Quarter the potatoes and add to crock pot. Peel the carrots and quarter them. Place the cut carrots into the crock pot. Peel and quarter the onion and place into the crock pot. Chop celery into medium-sized pieces and add to the crock pot. Cook for 6 to 7 hours. The stew will thicken over time.

Irish Sea Food Stew

Ingredients:

1	48 oz. can/box of vegetable or fish stock
1	small onion finely chopped
2	medium carrots chopped into small pieces
2	celery stalks chopped into small pieces
¼	pound of scallops, ¼ pound of crab meat, ¼ pound of cod (cubed) and ¼ pound of prawns cleaned and cubed (of course, you can use any seafood meat you like, add or take away).
	Salt
	Pepper
2	tbsps. of finely-chopped fennel

Directions:

Place a large stock pot on your stove and add all of the vegetable or fish stock to it. Bring the stock to a boil and add your onions, carrots and celery to the boiling stock. Turn the heat down to allow this to simmer for 20 to 30 minutes covered. Add your seafood, cover and allow it to simmer for about 10 minutes more. Taste and add salt and pepper to taste. Place in soup bowls and generously add the chopped fennel to each bowl as garnish.

Spinach Mashed Potatoes

Ingredients

8	large potatoes (russet potatoes are great for this recipe, but use white potatoes)
¼	pound of fresh spinach
1	pound of butter
4	tsps. salt
¼	tsp. pepper
½	cup heavy cream (may substitute milks from whole to skim)

Directions:

Peel and cut potatoes into 1-inch cubes and place in cold water with a pinch of salt. Bring the potatoes to a boil and then lower the heat to allow potatoes to cook at a simmer. You will know they are ready to mash when the potato will not stay on a fork when poked. While potatoes are boiling, in a frying pan add ½ a stick of butter (leave the rest for mashing the potatoes). Turn the heat on medium and melt the butter. Once the butter is melted, add the spinach and 2 tsps. of salt. Stir and cover. Let cook until the spinach is quite tender, stirring the spinach occasionally. Once the spinach is finished, set it aside. When the potatoes are finished, drain them completely of water. Add the remaining butter and salt. Using a hand masher, mash the potatoes to blend in the butter and salt. Using a hand mixer or stand mixer with the whip attachment, add cream and pepper. Whip on low until the cream is blended and then turn speed up to high. Turn mixer off. Drain the spinach of all liquid and add to potatoes. Mix the spinach into the potatoes with a spoon. Put the spinach potatoes into a serving bowl and serve.

Cheddar/Monterey Jack Cheese Buttermilk Biscuits

Ingredients

2	cups flour
¼	tsp. baking soda
1	tbsp. baking powder
1	tsp. salt
6	tbsps. butter cold
1	cup buttermilk
½	cup shredded Monterey Jack cheese
½	cup shredded medium cheddar cheese

Directions:

Preheat the oven to 450 degrees. Sift together the flour, baking soda, baking powder and salt. Cut the butter into cubes and add to the flour mixture. Mix this until it resembles a coarse meal. Add the buttermilk to the flour mixture and stir until combined. If the mixture appears to be dry, add 1 tbsp. of buttermilk at a time until it is at desired wetness. If too wet, add flour 1 tbsp. at a time until desired wetness. Finally, add the ½ cup of shredded Monterey Jack cheese and stir well. With a tablespoon scoop drop biscuit on a parchment covered cookie sheet. Place biscuits about 2 inches apart. Then take about 1 pinch of the cheddar cheese and place on top of each biscuit. Make sure that the tops are covered.

Bake for about 10-12 minutes - the biscuits will be a beautiful light golden brown on the top and bottom. Also, be sure cheese is golden brown. Some ovens cook unevenly. So, at about the 5- or 6-minute mark you should rotate the pan and finish cooking biscuits. Serve hot.

Chocolate Peanut Butter Cups

Ingredients:

1	cup peanut butter (smooth or crunchy)
2	cups confectioners' sugar
1	tsp. vanilla extract
14	oz. melting chocolate (use your favorite dark, milk or white chocolate)
2	tbsps. heavy cream
12	cupcake baking cups

Directions:

Mix peanut butter, confectioners' sugar, and vanilla extract until smooth. Set aside. Place cupcake baking cups in a cupcake pan. Melt chocolate in a double boiler over low heat. As the chocolate melts, add the 2 tbsps. heavy cream and stir. Watch constantly and stir often until melted. Remove from heat. With a spoon, pour melted chocolate on the bottom of a cupcake baking cup (enough to cover bottom and up about $\frac{1}{8}$-inch thick). Use a small spoon to take peanut butter mixture to place in cup. Using the chocolate spoon, pour chocolate over the peanut butter until it is covered completely. Repeat this for the remaining baking cups. Let stand to harden and serve. No need to refrigerate.

Cissy calling her friends to invite them over for a holiday celebration. These days she could just text them!

April

April brings spring showers, renewal and blossoms of hope. To celebrate the joyful times, cooks and families search for the freshest vegetables and fruits to complement their meals. A mélange of asparagus, peas and crisp beans topped with mint is a nod to the greenery of the month. A search for the most succulent ham recipe adds to the fun of the season as well anticipating the hunt for colorful hidden Easter eggs. Following are three menus and recipes to make "every bunny" proud.

Easter Brunch

Appetizer
Mom's Deviled Eggs

Entrée
Plum Glazed Ham
Roasted Asparagus
Potato Salad
Hot Cross Buns

Dessert
Easter Bunny Cake

Easter Dinner

First Course
Avgolemono Soup

Entrée
Garlic Roasted Chicken with Apples and Shallots
Fresh Green Beans and Shallots
Golden Potatoes

Dessert
Carrot Cake

Easter Dinner

First Course
Swedish Pancakes with Crème Fraiche and Dill

Entrée
Seared Salmon with Avocado Sauce
Cucumber Salad
Boiled New Potatoes
Bread Basket

Dessert
Strawberry Trifle

Recipes

Moms Deviled Eggs

Ingredients

6	large eggs (makes 12 deviled halves)
2	tbsps. Best Foods mayonnaise
1½	tsps. Dijon mustard
1	tsp. truffle aioli
¼	tsp. dill
	Sea salt
	Lemon pepper
	Paprika for sprinkling

Choice of toppings

¼	tsp. of black caviar per egg
	Real bacon bits
	Half sliced green or black olives
	Sliced chives

Directions

Place eggs in a medium saucepan. Cover with cold water. Bring to a boil then cover and remove from heat. Let stand for 7-8 minutes. Drain and place pan in refrigerator for five minutes. Pour cold water over eggs. Remove eggs one at a time; crack on either end of the egg, and then roll to crack further. Peel the eggs.

Slice eggs in half lengthwise. Pop the yolks out of white into medium bowl. Mash yolks into small crumbles. Add Best Foods mayonnaise, Dijon mustard, aioli, dill, salt and lemon pepper. Mix thoroughly.

With small spoon, mound mixture into the whites. Sprinkle with paprika and add your favorite topping. This will serve 12 people.

Plum Glazed Baked Ham

Ingredients
- 1   3-4 lb. bone-in ham
- 1   10 oz. jar plum jam (about 1 cup)
- ¼   cup pomegranate juice
- ⅛   tsp. ground cloves
- 1   tbsp. Dijon mustard

Directions
Preheat oven to 350 degrees F. Line a roasting pan with foil. Place a roasting rack in the pan and put ham on the rack. When temperature is ready, roast the ham for 45 minutes without cover.

Stir together the jam, pomegranate juice and cloves in a small saucepan. Heat over low until the mixture is melted. Spoon half of the sauce over the ham and tent with foil. Roast for 1 to 1½ hours more or until internal temperature reaches 140 degrees.

When finished roasting, let stand for 10 minutes, covered. Stir mustard into remaining jam mixture and heat through. To serve, place ham on a platter and pour heated sauce over the ham.

Roasted Asparagus

Ingredients

1	lb. thick asparagus
2	tbsps. olive oil
1½	tbsps. Parmesan cheese, grated
2	cloves minced garlic
	Kosher salt
	White pepper
	Lemon juice or balsamic vinegar

Directions

Preheat oven to 400 degrees F. Rinse and dry the asparagus spears. Snap and discard tough ends. Place the spears into a mixing bowl and drizzle with the olive oil. Toss to coat them and then sprinkle with Parmesan cheese, garlic, salt, and pepper.

Roast in oven 10 minutes until the asparagus are lightly brown and tender.

Sprinkle with lemon juice or balsamic vinegar and serve.

Potato Salad

Ingredients

3	lbs. of small white potatoes
	Salt
1¼	cup Best Foods mayonnaise
2	tbsps. Dijon Mustard
2	tbsps. whole grain mustard
½	cup fresh dill, chopped
1	tbsp. sugar
1	tsp. sea salt
	White pepper
1	tsp. garlic powder
2	celery ribs sliced
½	cup red onion, chopped
3	hardboiled eggs

Directions

Place potatoes in large pot of water. Add salt. Bring to a boil then simmer over low heat for 10 to fifteen minutes or until potatoes are tender when you pierce them with a knife.

Drain the potatoes in a colander and then place the colander with the potatoes over the large pot, cover and let steam for 15 minutes.

For the dressing: in a bowl mix together the mayonnaise, two mustards, dill, sugar, salt, pepper and garlic powder.

Cut potatoes in half or quarters. Place warm potatoes in a large bowl and pour the dressing over them. Add the onion and celery, salt and pepper. Mix well. Add the eggs, then cover and refrigerate.

Hot Cross Buns

With all the activities at Easter, here is an easy way to make hot cross buns!

Ingredients

8	refrigerated buttermilk biscuits (one package)
1	tsp. ground cinnamon
1	tsp. brown sugar, packed down
½	cup currants
1	egg, lightly beaten
5	tbsps. confectioners' sugar
1	tsp. water

Directions

Preheat oven to 350 degrees F. Open and then place refrigerated biscuits on a board or plate. Stretch each biscuit into a four-inch circle. Mix the brown sugar and cinnamon in a small bowl. Sprinkle ¼ tsp. of the sugar mixture a 1 tbsp. of currants over half of each biscuit. Fold over the plain biscuit half onto the currant half. Fold again, and pinch the edges to seal. Shape each biscuit into a ball. Place and evenly space buns in a lightly greased 9-inch cake pan. Brush bun tops with the beaten egg.

Bake 15-10 minutes or until golden brown. Remove buns onto cooling rack. Cool completely.

Avgolemono Soup

Ingredients

- 8 cups chicken broth
- 1 cup orzo pasta
- 3 eggs
- 1 lemon, juiced
- Salt
- Flat leaf parsley for garnish

Directions

Bring broth to boil in large saucepan. Add orzo.

Cover and cook on medium low heat for 15 minutes. While the rice cooks, lightly beat the eggs and the lemon juice together.

Remove the broth from heat. Slowly mix about one cup of the hot broth into the egg lemon mixture. Add to the soup gradually while stirring.

Place pan back on the heat, and stir until soup is heated through (do not boil).

Spoon into bowls and garnish with flat-leaf parsley.

Roasted Chicken with Apples and Shallots

Ingredients

2	apples cored and quartered.
12	shallots, peeled
1	bunch thyme
2	tbsps. olive oil, divided
1	3-4 lb. chicken, rinsed and patted dry with paper towel
	Salt and pepper

Directions

Preheat oven to 400 degrees F. Place apples, 10 shallots and half the thyme in the bottom of large roasting pan. Drizzle the mixture with 1 tablespoon of the olive oil and season with kosher salt and cracked pepper. Push apples and shallots mixture to edges of pan.

Place remaining shallots and thyme in the body of the chicken and tie legs of chicken together with kitchen twine. Place chicken in the center of the roasting pan and rub all over with remaining olive oil and season liberally with salt and pepper. Place in the oven and roast about 90 minutes or until internal temperature reaches 160 degrees.

Fresh Green Beans and Shallots

Ingredients

4	cups water
1	lb. small French green beans, cleaned and snipped
3	tbsps. shallots, peeled of outer and inner skins, chopped
	Salt and pepper to taste
1	tsp. lemon juice

Directions

In a medium saucepan, bring water to a boil. Add the beans and cover. Cook for 3-5 minutes until tender. Drain and rinse the beans under cold water.

Melt butter in a medium fry pan over low-medium heat. Add the shallots and sauté for about one minute until the shallots begin to brown. Add the beans, salt and pepper and sauté quickly. Sprinkle with the lemon juice and serve with the chicken.

Golden Potatoes

Ingredients

6   (about 1¼ lbs.) Golden Yukon potatoes, cut in wedges
6   cloves of garlic left whole in skin
1   tbsp. fresh rosemary leaves, chopped
3   tbsps. extra virgin olive oil
     Salt and freshly-ground pepper to taste

Directions

Preheat oven to 425 degrees F. On a baking sheet place the potato wedges. Toss with garlic, rosemary, and oil. Sprinkle with salt and pepper. Arrange potato cut side down in a single layer and roast until fork tender, about 20-25 minutes

Carrot Cake

Ingredients

Cake

1	cup pecans
2	cups all-purpose flour
2	tsps. baking powder
2	tsps. baking soda
1	tsp. cinnamon
1	tsp. salt
¾	cup vegetable oil
½	cup buttermilk
1½	tsps. vanilla extract
4	large eggs
2	cups sugar
1	lb. carrots, peeled and coarsely shredded

Frosting

½	lb. (2 sticks) unsalted butter
2	two 8 oz. packages, cream cheese, softened
1	tsp. vanilla extract
2	cups confectioners' sugar

Directions

Preheat oven to 325 degrees F. Butter two 9-inch cake pans. Flour the pans and shake off excess flour.

Spread the pecans on a baking sheet and toast for 7-8 minutes until golden brown. Cool and then finely chop the pecans.

Whisk the flour, baking powder, baking soda, cinnamon and salt in a medium bowl. In a small bowl, whisk the oil, buttermilk and vanilla. In the large bowl of an electric mixer, beat the eggs and sugar at high speed about 5 minutes. Beat in the liquid ingredients. Then beat in the dry ingredients until just moistened. Stir in the carrots and pecans. Divide the batter between the pans and bake the cakes for 55 minutes to one hour until golden. Let the cake cool on a rack for 30 minutes. Invert the cakes and let cool completely.

Beat the butter and cream cheese at high speed in an electric mixer. Then, beat in the vanilla and then the confectioners' sugar. Beat at low speed until incorporated. Increase the speed to high and beat until light and fluffy, about 3 minutes. On one cake layer spread a cup of the frosting. Top with second layer right side up. Spread the top and sides with the remaining frosting and cool in the refrigerator until chilled about one hour. Slice and serve.

Swedish Pancakes

Ingredients

6	eggs
2½	cups milk
1½	cups flour
2	tbsps. sugar
½	tsp. vanilla
	Pinch of salt
	Butter for greasing
	Powdered sugar
	Fresh blueberries

Directions

Whisk all ingredients except butter together until the batter is smooth and well combined.

Heat a 9" cast-iron pan over medium heat. When the pan is very hot, melt the butter in the pan. Pour ⅓ cup of the batter in a circular motion into the hot pan. When the pancake starts to have a lot of bubbles, flip it.

Use a thin spatula to separate the pancake from the pan. Stack the pancakes to keep them warm. Roll the pancakes to serve them. Place on plate. Sprinkle powdered sugar and blueberries on top of pancakes for a delicious first course!

Seared Salmon with Avocado Sauce

Ingredients

1-1½ lbs. salmon fillets
    Grapeseed or olive oil
2   large avocados, cut and peeled
3   tbsps. fresh lemon or lime juice
3-4   tbsps. extra virgin olive oil
1   tbsp. minced shallot or green onion
1   tbsp. parsley, minced
1   tsp. Dijon mustard
    Salt and pepper to taste

Directions

Make avocado sauce: Place avocado pieces and lemon or lime juice into a blender or food processor and pulse until blended. Slowly add olive oil, with blender on, until desired consistency of sauce is reached. Add minced shallot and parsley, and pulse until just combined. Set aside.

Sauté the salmon fillets. Coat the bottom of a sauté pan with the oil on medium-high heat. Season both sides of the salmon fillets with salt and pepper, then carefully lay the salmon in the pan, skin side down. Cook the salmon until about medium doneness, about 3-4 minutes per side. Top the salmon with the sauce and some clipped parsley and serve.

Boiled Potatoes

Ingredients

1	lb. small new potatoes
1	head garlic, halved crosswise
1	bay leaf
1	tsp. black peppercorns
	Kosher salt
2-4	tbsps. unsalted butter
	Freshly-ground pepper

Directions

Into a large saucepan put the potatoes, garlic, bay leaf and peppercorns. Add cold water to cover about an inch and season generously with salt. Bring to a boil, lower the heat and simmer until the potatoes are tender, about 5-8 minutes. Drain and discard the garlic, bay leaves and peppercorns. Halve the potatoes. Toss with the butter and season with salt and pepper to taste. Keep warm until served. This will serve 4.

Cucumber Salad

Ingredients

2	English cucumbers, thinly sliced
1	tsp. salt
1	red onion, thinly sliced
1	cup distilled white vinegar
½	cup water
½	cup granulated sugar
2	tbsps. fresh dill, minced

Directions

Season the cucumbers with salt in a large bowl and place in the refrigerator for 1 hour or more. Drain liquids and lightly squeeze cucumbers, then toss with onion slices.

In a small saucepan over high heat, pour in white vinegar and water and stir in sugar until dissolved and liquid turns clear, about 3-5 minutes.

Pour liquid over cucumber and onions; stir in dill. Cover with plastic wrap and refrigerate 1 hour. Serve cold or at room temperature. This will serve 8 people.

Strawberry Trifle

Ingredients

1	cup cold milk
1	cup sour cream
1	package (3.4 oz.) instant vanilla pudding mix
1	tsp. grated orange zest
2	cups heavy whipping cream, whipped
8	cups cubed angel food cake
4	cups sliced fresh strawberries

Directions

In a large bowl, beat the milk, sour cream, pudding mix and orange zest on low speed until thickened. Fold in whipped cream. Place half of the cake cubes in a 3-quart glass bowl. Arrange a third of the strawberries around the sides of the bowl and over the cake. Top with half of the pudding mixture. Repeat layers once. Top with remaining berries.

Serves 10.

Refrigerate for 2 hours before serving and enjoy!

Kathy's Baby Lettuce Salad with glazed walnuts, cranberries and pear.

May

THIS MONTH HOLDS TWO special holidays: Mother's Day and Memorial Day. You will find menus for both of these days. I always love May; it is the signal that summer is just around the corner. I loved my summers!

Mother's Day seems to be the day that most people I know take their moms out for a very nice brunch, lunch or dinner. That is great. But I am going to include a Mother's Day menu that I think most moms would love for their families to make for them. It is such a great time to show how much you have learned from your mother and how much you love her. What a better gift than the gift of your presence?

Memorial Day was that first holiday of the year that signals summer. I understood the holiday and what it meant. I had a couple of relatives that served in the armed forces and we always recognized those who served and gave their lives for our freedoms. This holiday was always celebrated picnic-style. There is a special recipe in this chapter that was handed down through my maternal grandfather's family. It is a special macaroni salad that has bananas in it. I know that sounds weird, but if you like bananas you are going to have to try this recipe. Like I said earlier, experiment with your food. Try it! If you don't like it, leave the bananas out next time.

Mother's Day (Beef, Pork, Chicken or Fish)

Appetizer
Caprese Salad

First Course
Almond and Fresh Green Bean Salad

Entrée
Grilled/Oven Roasted Peppered Steak,
Pork or Chicken Kabobs or
Lemon and Rosemary Seared Salmon
Vegetable Skewers

Dessert
Chocolate-covered Strawberries
with Champagne Whipped Cream

Scot's Caprese Salad.

Memorial Day Beef, Chicken, Pork or Fish

Appetizer
Bruschetta

First Course
Fresh Fruit Salad

Entrée
BBQ Tri-Tip,
BBQ Pork Chop,
BBQ Chicken,
BBQ Shark Steak
Macaroni Salad
Grilled Garlic Corn on the Cob

Dessert
Caramel Brownies

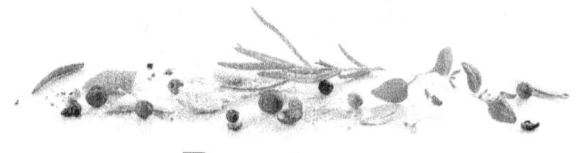

Recipes

Caprese Salad

Ingredients

- 2   beef steak tomatoes
- 1   ball of fresh mozzarella cheese
-      Fresh basil leaves
-      Salt
-      Pepper
-      ⅛ cup of balsamic vinegar
-      ⅛ cup of olive oil

Directions

Evenly slice the tomatoes and mozzarella cheese. Begin to place them on a platter in the following pattern: tomato, mozzarella, tomato, mozzarella until you run out of each.* Put a pinch of salt and a pinch of pepper over the entire dish. Mix the olive oil and balsamic vinegar together and then drizzle over the dish and serve. If you need to serve later, do not drizzle the balsamic and olive oil mixture until you are ready. You can keep it refrigerated until you are ready to drizzle and serve.

*Note: Do not stack but overlay the tomato and mozzarella.

Almond and Fresh Green Bean Salad

Ingredients

1	pound of fresh green beans cleaned and ends removed
½	cup sliced almonds
1	fresh lemon
1	tbsp. olive oil
1	tbsp. balsamic vinegar
	Pinch of salt
	Pinch of pepper

Directions

Blanch the green beans and then dry them thoroughly! Over medium heat, add the olive oil, green beans, salt, and pepper. Sauté the beans and at the last minute add the balsamic vinegar and toss the beans around for about a minute. Drain off the excess oil and vinegar and place in a serving dish. Zest the lemon and set aside the zest. Squeeze the juice of the lemon over the beans. In another pan, put the sliced almonds in and heat over medium heat. This will toast them and bring out the flavor more. Toss them in this pan for about a minute. Sprinkle the sliced almonds over the beans and sprinkle some of the zest over that. Serve.

Grilled/Oven Roasted Peppered Steak, Pork or Chicken

Ingredients

2	lbs. sirloin steak, 2 lbs. boneless pork chops, or 2 pounds of cubed chicken (breast or thigh)
½	cup coarse pepper
	Salt
1	cup olive oil
1	cup apple cider vinegar
	Package of skewers

Directions

Mix oil and vinegar. Cut the meat into cubes and place in a bowl. Pour half the mixture of oil and vinegar into the bowl. Cover the bowls and refrigerate for 1 hour. After the hour is up, drain the meat. Place the meat on skewers. Spread the ½ cup of coarse pepper on a cookie sheet. Roll the skewered meat in the pepper. Sprinkle salt over all the meat. Grill all sides for 8 minutes. Make sure to get good grill marks. If you are baking, bake in a 375-degree oven for 25 minutes. Rotate the meat at the halfway mark. Serve hot. Make sure your meat is up to temperature. You do not want to serve any meat undercooked.

*Note: Follow these directions no matter what meat you are using.

Lemon and Rosemary Seared Salmon

Ingredients

1	salmon steak per guest
2	lemons
	Fresh rosemary
	Salt
	Pepper
	Olive oil

Directions

Place 2 tablespoons of olive oil in a frying pan and set aside. Place your salmon steaks out on cutting boards. Lightly salt and pepper both sides. Zest both lemons and set that aside. Juice both lemons and set aside. Take one sprig of rosemary for each salmon steak and set aside. Turn the stove to high and place your frying pan on the heat. Once the oil is hot, place your salmon steaks in the pan and sear each side for about one minute. Remove from the heat. Pour the lemon juice over all the salmon steaks, sprinkle the lemon zest over the top of the salmon steaks and add one sprig of rosemary to each steak. Cover and let sit for about 2 to 5 minutes before serving.

Vegetable Skewers

Ingredients

3   medium red potatoes thoroughly washed and dried
1   yellow bell pepper
1   green bell pepper
1   red bell pepper
1   basket of whole button mushrooms
1   medium sweet onion
1   basket of cherry tomatoes
    Salt
    Garlic
2   sticks of butter melted or ⅔ cup olive oil
1   package of skewers

Directions

Cut the potatoes into large cubes. Place them in a bowl with about 3 tablespoons of melted butter or olive oil. Add a teaspoon of salt and a teaspoon of garlic. Mix well and place the cubes on a skewer. Place the skewers on a grill and grill at medium heat until golden brown and tender or place on parchment paper-covered cookie sheet and bake in a 400-degree oven for about 20 minutes or until golden brown and tender. While the potatoes are cooking, cut the tops of all the peppers and remove the seeds. Then cut each pepper into 8 even pieces. Wash and dry the mushrooms. Peel and quarter the onion. Then, cut each of the quarters in half. Wash and dry the cherry tomatoes. Fill each skewer with the vegetables. You can do the following pattern until skewer is full: Yellow bell pepper, mushroom, tomato, green bell pepper, onion, red bell pepper and start over until skewer is full. Set the skewers aside. Mix 1 tsp. salt and 1 tsp. garlic into the melted butter. With pastry brush, coat all sides of the vegetables with the butter. If you can grill, place them on the grill rotating every couple of minutes until all have char marks. If you are using an oven, place the skewered vegetables on a parchment-covered cookie sheet and bake in a 400-degree oven for 5 minutes, rotate and leave another 5 minutes. Check your skewers at the first 5 minutes; you might not need the other 5 minutes. Serve hot!

Chocolate-covered Strawberries with Champagne Whipped Cream

Ingredients

12   fresh strawberries (or as many as you need for your guests)

8   oz. of chocolate for melting (use your favorite dark, milk or white chocolate)

Champagne Whipped Cream (recipe on next page)

Directions

Wash and dry the strawberries thoroughly. Set the berries aside. Melt chocolate in a double boiler over low heat. Watch constantly and stir often until melted. Remove from heat. Pick the strawberry up by the stem and dip in the chocolate and place on wax paper. Repeat until all strawberries are done. Place the strawberries in the refrigerator until you are ready to serve. Place on a nice serving tray and place the champagne whipped cream in the center.

Champagne Whipped Cream

Ingredients

1	cup of heavy whipping cream
¼	cup of confectioners' sugar
¼	cup of champagne
1	tsp. vanilla extract

Directions

Using a mixer, whip heavy cream in a stand mixer. (It is always good to have placed your mixing bowl in the freezer for a few minutes before you whip the cream.) Whip until nice peaks start to form. Add the sugar and vanilla and continue to whip for a few seconds. Add the champagne and whip until mixed and the peaks stay. Place in refrigerator until you are ready to use.

Simple Bruschetta

Ingredients

1	baguette
3	tomatoes
	Fresh oregano
	Fresh grated mozzarella
3	tbsps. butter
1	tsp. of garlic powder

Directions

Slice the baguette into ¼-inch slices. Melt the butter and add the garlic powder. Use a pastry brush to add the garlic butter to each slice of bruschetta. Toast the bruschetta in an oven at 425 degrees until golden brown. While bread is cooling, dice tomatoes, chop fresh oregano and grate ½ cup of mozzarella. Once bread is cooled, top with tomatoes, oregano and mozzarella. Bake in a 475-degree oven until cheese is melted. Remove it from the oven and immediately plate it and serve it.

Fresh Fruit Salad

Ingredients

1	pint strawberries
1	pint blueberries
1	bunch of seedless grapes (your choice of grape)
1	tbsp. sugar (optional)

Directions

Rinse and dry all fruit before starting. Cut the tops off the strawberries and then slice them and place them in a serving bowl. Put the whole blueberries in the bowl. Slice the grapes in half and add to the bowl. Sprinkle the sugar over the top and mix the fruit (this is optional). Chill until ready to serve.

BBQ Tri-Tip/BBQ Pork Chop/ BBQ Chicken

Ingredients

    Tri-tip roast (enough for guests and you can have butcher slice into steaks), chicken (buy the pieces that your guests like to eat. Just be sure it gets cooked to temperature)

- ¼ cup of honey
- 1 16 oz. can of tomato sauce
- 1 8 oz. can of tomato paste
- ¼ cup of apple cider vinegar
- 2 tbsps. Sriracha sauce
- 2 tbsps. of Worcestershire sauce
- 2 tsps. garlic powder
- 2 tsps. paprika
- 2 tsps. salt
- 1 tsp. mustard powder

Directions

Keep your meat refrigerated until you finish making the BBQ sauce. Place all of the other ingredients in a large mixing bowl. Mix together until well blended. Take about ¼ of a cup out and leave in the refrigerator until you are ready to grill. Place your meat in the sauce you just made to marinate for at least 30 minutes (but not more than 2 hours). Then you can grill to your liking. Use the set aside BBQ sauce to brush on each side of the steaks, chops or chicken as you cook.*

*Note: Follow this recipe no matter what meat you have chosen to cook.

BBQ Shark Steak

Ingredients

    Shark steaks (Get enough for guests. I would go to a store specializing in seafood. In a pinch, you can use frozen.)

3	tsps. cayenne pepper
1	tsp. salt
1	tsp. lemon pepper
1	tsp. garlic powder
1	tsp. thyme
2	fresh lemons for garnish

Directions

Place the cayenne pepper, salt, lemon pepper, garlic powder, and thyme in a bowl. Mix this well. You will use this as a dry rub on your steaks before you grill them. Let the rub sit on each steak for about 5 to ten minutes before you grill them. When you are ready to grill, make sure the grill is well oiled and then cook the shark steaks on medium heat for 5-6 minutes per side or until the flesh is flaky. Garnish each steak with a lemon slice.

Macaroni Salad

Ingredients

1   lb. package of elbow macaroni, any size
6   hardboiled eggs peeled and cooled
1   16 oz. jar of sweet pickles
1   large sweet onion
1   32 oz. jar of Miracle Whip
    Salt
    Pepper
6   bananas (optional)

Directions

Boil the macaroni to al dente, rinse with cold water and place in a mixing bowl. Quarter the eggs and then cut the quarters into quarters and place in with the macaroni. Quarter the sweet pickles and then quarter those and place in the bowl with the macaroni. Peel and dice the onion. Place that into the bowl with the macaroni. Add half the jar of Miracle Whip and mix. If it doesn't coat everything nicely, add a tablespoon more until all coats nicely. Add salt and pepper to taste. Refrigerate. If you are going to add bananas, you will do the next step just before serving: Slice the bananas into small bowl. Use half a lemon and squeeze the juice from the lemon over the bananas and stir.* Drain off excess juice and add the bananas to the salad. Stir in the bananas and serve cold.

*Note: The lemon juice helps keep the bananas from turning brown.

Garlic Corn on the Cob

Ingredients

    Corn on the cob (enough so that everyone gets at least one)
2   sticks of butter
3   cloves of garlic
    Salt
    Pepper

Directions

Preheat your oven to 400 degrees. Shuck and rinse your corn on the cob. Set that aside to let it dry while you make your butter. Use a small saucepan and melt the butter. While butter is melting, put your 3 cloves of garlic through a garlic press. Once the butter is melted, add the garlic and stir. Let this cook on low heat for about 2 minutes and then remove it from the heat. Add 1 tsp. of salt and 1 tsp. of pepper and stir it again. Let it sit for about 20 minutes. After it has sat for the 20 minutes, use a pastry brush and cover each cob with the infused butter. Wrap each cob in foil and place on the middle rack of your 400-degree oven and let cook for about 30 minutes. Then you can remove it and serve.

Caramel Brownies

Ingredients

½	cup butter, room temperature
¾	cup sugar
2	eggs
1	tsp. vanilla
¾	cup of flour
¼	cup of dark chocolate cocoa powder
1	tsp. salt
½	cup cold water
10	unwrapped caramels

Directions

Preheat the oven to 325 degrees. Mix the butter until creamy. Add the sugar and cream together. Add 2 eggs and mix well. Add 1 tsp. of vanilla and mix well. Set this aside and sift together all the dry ingredients. Mix in the dry ingredients with the wet (¼ at a time). Hand mix in the 10 caramels to the batter. Grease and flour a 9x13" baking pan. Bake for 20-25 minutes or until a toothpick poked into the center comes out clean. Great served warm or cold and with a scoop of your favorite ice cream.

Kathy and Scot during a shoot with Kathy making her Spinach and Artichoke Dip.

June

GRADUATION AND FATHER'S DAY highlight the warmth of the new month. Tasseled youths look forward to a new stage in their life as celebrations add to their enjoyment. The time to celebrate Dad is not to have him barbecue. Maybe it's time for that newly graduated student to take charge of the charcoals or give those hamburgers some stripes on the gas grill. Maybe Mom can stir up some paternal favorites. Whatever it is, the events are a family affair whether they are celebrated by one grad or all those who create a culinary tribute to their special father or to the father that raised us all.

Father's Day Barbecue (Meat)

Appetizer
Spinach and Artichoke Dip

Assorted Crackers

Entrée
Barbecued Hamburgers and Hot Dogs

Buns

Condiments

Grilled Corn with Sour Cream and Cotija Cheese

Sliced Tomatoes

Dessert
Watermelon

Brownies

Father's Day Casual Dinner (Fish)

Appetizer
Warm Ricotta Cheese Dip with pine nuts, olives and raisins

Entrée
Beer Batter Fish

French Fries

Cabbage Salad

Dessert
Jamoca Almond Fudge Ice Cream with Hot Fudge

Cookies

Graduation Dinner

First Course
Strawberry and Beet Salad with
Chevre Dressing Vinaigrette

Entrée
Dijon Roasted Rack of Lamb
Eggplant Sauté
Couscous

Dessert
Lemon Cups

Recipes

Spinach and Artichoke Dip

Ingredients

- ¼ cup mayonnaise
- 1 (8 oz.) package cream cheese, softened
- ¼ cup fresh Romano cheese, grated
- ¼ fresh Parmesan cheese, grated
- 1 clove garlic, peeled and minced
- ½ tsp. dried basil
- Salt and pepper to taste
- ½ cup frozen chopped spinach, thawed and drained
- 1 (14 oz.) can artichoke hearts, drained and chopped

Directions

Preheat oven to 350 degrees F. Lightly grease a small baking dish. Mix together mayonnaise, cream cheese, Romano cheese, Parmesan cheese, garlic, basil, salt and pepper in a medium bowl. Gently stir in the artichoke hearts and spinach.

Transfer the mixture to the prepared baking dish. Bake in the preheated oven 25 minutes until bubbly. Serve with sturdy tortilla chips and crackers.

Barbecued Hamburgers

Ingredients

1	pound of hamburger meat
2	tbsps. barbecue rub
4	onion or sesame hamburger buns
1	tbsp. or more or olive oil
4	slices bacon
4	thick slices red ripe tomatoes
6	tbsps. of your favorite barbecue sauce

Directions

Form the hamburger meat into 4 patties. Make an indentation in the middle of each patty. This allows the beef to cook more evenly. Marinate the burgers with the rub and place in the refrigerator until the grill is ready.

Set the grill to high and preheat, brush and oil the grill grate. Brush the onion or sesame seed buns on the inside with olive oil. Place the bacon strip on the grate and grill until browned on both sides about 3 minutes. Place the hamburger meat on the grill and cook for about 4 minutes per side for medium rare. When done, place the burger on the oiled bun, spread with barbecue sauce, then tomato slice and bacon. Top with the other roll half.

Grilled Corn on the Cob

Ingredients

4	ears of corn
	Garlic butter
¼	cup grated cotija cheese
2	fresh limes, quartered
1	tbsp. chives, chopped for garnish

Directions

Make the garlic butter: combine butter, garlic and chives in a food processor or mash until smooth. Season the butter with the salt and pepper. Set aside until ready to use.

Preheat grill to medium.

Peel the husks back from the corn and remove the silks. Raise the husks back up to cover the corn. Soak the corn in a large bowl in cold water for about 30 minutes. Take the corn out of the cold bath and shake off the excess water. Put the corn on the cob on the grill, close the cover and let cook for about fifteen minutes.

When done, carefully unwrap the corn cobs and brush with the garlic butter. Sprinkle the cotija cheese over the butter and squeeze with lime. Sprinkle with chopped chives to garnish.

Vegetable Platter with Ranch Dressing

Ingredients

For the Dip

1	pint sour cream
2	cups mayonnaise
1	tbsp. dill weed
1	tbsp. Italian herb mix
1½	tbsps. salt
½	tbsp. black pepper
2	tbsp. sugar
½	cup lemon juice

For the Platter

- Green leaf lettuce (to line the platter)
- Baby carrots
- 1 lb. broccoli crowns
- 1-2 cucumbers
- Small sticks of celery
- Red Pepper
- Red cabbage, hallowed out, to hold the dressing

Directions

In a medium bowl mix together the sour cream, mayonnaise, dill weed, Italian herbs, salt and pepper plus the sugar and lemon juice. Set aside in the refrigerator.

Rub the tops of the broccoli crowns with a little olive oil. Score the cucumbers lengthwise with the tines of a fork; cut into ½" slices.

Wash the celery sticks. Cut the red peppers in half. Take out the seeds and then cut into ¼-inch slices.

To assemble platter, line the platter with lettuce leaves. Place the hallowed-out cabbage in the center of the tray. Surround the cabbage with broccoli crowns, and then set the vegetables around the broccoli in a pinwheel pattern. Spoon the dressing from the bowl from the refrigerator into the cabbage and serve.

Katharine Hepburn's Brownies

In a tip of the culinary hat, following here is Katharine's own recipe for delicious gooey brownies!

Ingredients

- ½ cup cocoa
- ½ cup butter (1 stick)
- 1 cup sugar
- ¼ cup flour
- 1 cup walnuts, broken up or chopped or pecans
- 1 tsp. vanilla
- Pinch of salt

Directions

Preheat oven to 325 degrees F. Melt butter in saucepan with cocoa and stir until smooth. Remove from heat and allow cooling for a few minutes, and then transfer to a large bowl. Whisk in eggs, one at a time. Stir in vanilla.

In a separate bowl, combine sugar, flour, nuts and salt. Add to the cocoa-butter mixture; stir until just combined. Pour into a greased 8x8-inch square pan. Bake 30-35 minutes. Do not over bake; the brownies should be gooey. Let cool, then cut into bars.

Thanks, Katharine!

Strawberry and Beet Salad with Chèvre

Ingredients

8	cups mixed baby greens
4	small red beets, cooked and chopped
4	oz. chèvre goat cheese
½	cup strawberries
2	oz. glazed pecans

For the honey balsamic vinaigrette

2	tbsps. balsamic vinegar
2	tbsps. extra virgin olive oil
1	tbsp. honey

Directions

Whisk olive oil, balsamic, and honey together in a small bowl. Place greens in a large bowl, toss with vinaigrette and mix well. Divide between four plates. Top each salad with beets, goat cheese, strawberries and pecans.

Dijon Roasted Rack of Lamb

Ingredients

	Rack of lamb (7-8 bones)
1	tsp. salt
1	tsp. pepper
2	tbsps. garlic olive oil
1	tbsp. Dijon mustard
½	cup fresh bread crumbs
2	tbsps. minced garlic
2	tbsps. fresh rosemary, chopped
1	tsp. salt
¼	tsp. black pepper
2	tbsps. olive oil

Directions

Put oven rack in center position. Preheat the oven to 450 degrees F. Combine bread crumbs, garlic, rosemary, salt and pepper in a large bowl. Moisten the mixture with 2 tbsps. of the olive oil. Set aside.

Season the rack of lamb with salt and pepper. Over high heat 2 tbsps. of the garlic olive oil in a large ovenproof skillet. Sear rack of lamb for 1-2 minutes on all sides. Set aside to briefly cool, and then brush the rack with Dijon mustard. Roll the rack in the bread crumb mixture until evenly coated. Cover the ends of the rib bones with foil to prevent blackening.

Arrange the rack, bone side up, in the large skillet. Roast the lamb in the oven for 12-18 minutes. Let it rest for 5-7 minutes loosely covered before carving between the ribs and serving.

Eggplant Sauté

Ingredients

1-2	large eggplant (about two pounds)
2	cups chopped ripe tomatoes
	Salt and pepper to taste
⅓	cup olive oil
1½	tbsps. minced garlic
	Chopped fresh parsley

Directions

Peel the eggplant and cut into slices and then 1-inch cubes. Place the eggplant in a colander and sprinkle liberally with salt. Let the cubes sit for at least thirty minutes.

Squeeze out the liquid, rinse with fresh water and pat dry.

Heat a large nonstick skillet over medium heat and cover the bottom with the olive oil. Add ½ tsp. of garlic. Sauté for 2 minutes and then add eggplant. Stir occasionally until the eggplant is tender and lightly browned, about 15 minutes.

Stir in the tomatoes and cook for about ten minutes, stirring occasionally. Add the rest of the garlic and cook, stirring for about one minute. Add more salt and pepper, if desired. Stir in a handful of parsley.

Serve hot, warm or at room temperature, with the lamb and couscous.

Couscous

Ingredients

¼	cup butter
1	yellow onion, thinly sliced
1-2	cloves garlic, crushed
1	cup couscous
2	cups chicken stock
2	tbsps. parsley, chopped
	Salt and pepper to taste

Directions

Melt butter in a heavy medium saucepan. Add sliced onions, stir and cook until soft about ten minutes. Stir in crushed garlic. Slowly add couscous and stir until well blended. Add chicken stock, stir all ingredients and bring to boil. Remove from heat. Cover and allow to stand for five minutes. Stir in parsley. Then salt and pepper to taste.

Lemon Cups

Ingredients

½	cup sugar
2	tbsps. cornstarch
1	cup cold water
¼	cup fresh lemon juice
1	large egg
½	tsp. lemon peel, grated
1	tsp. unsalted butter

Phyllo Cups

	Nonstick oil spray
4	sheets phyllo dough, fresh or frozen (thawed)
1	tbsp. unsalted butter, melted
1	tsp. sugar
½	tsp. powdered sugar
	Raspberries for decoration

Directions

Custard

Whisk sugar, cornstarch and salt together in a heavy medium saucepan. Gradually whisk in 1 cup cold water and the lemon juice. Whisk together until sugar and cornstarch dissolve. Then whisk in egg and lemon peel. Add the butter. Whisk over medium heat until mixture boils and thickens, about 5 minutes. Remove from heat. Transfer custard to medium bowl and press plastic wrap onto surface of custard. Cool to room temperature.

Phyllo Cups

Preheat oven to 375 degrees F. Lightly spray eight ⅓-cup muffin cups with vegetable oil spray. Stack four phyllo sheets into six 4-inch squares, making a total of 24 squares. Press 1 phyllo square into each muffin cup. Cover remaining phyllo with plastic wrap and damp towel. Using pastry brush, dab phyllo in a few places with melted butter. Press another phyllo square on top of first phyllo square with corners at different angles. Sprinkle the cups with phyllo with sugar.

Bake the cups in the preheated oven until the phyllo is golden brown, about 6 minutes. Transfer pan to rack and cool. Remove cups from pan and spoon some of the custard into each of the cups to fill. Top each cup with a raspberry and enjoy!

Scot's Strawberry Shortcake.

July

Summer is in full swing and time to celebrate the birth of our nation. The 4th of July is one of my favorite times of the year. My childhood was filled with camping trips to the Oregon coast and fireworks! It was also a time for exploring with friends. The joys of camping in my youth were campfires and toasting marshmallows. Spending time and sharing food with family and good friends was always on the agenda.

I have included a potato salad recipe that was given to me by my mother. It is a sweeter potato salad than most are used to being served. It is pretty much the same as the macaroni salad, minus the bananas and potatoes instead of macaroni. Enjoy!

July 4th Beef, Chicken, Pork or Fish

Appetizer
Jalapeño Corn Bread Poppers

First Course
Cucumber Onion Salad

Entrée
Inside Out Cheese Burger,
Ground Pork Burger,
Spicy Chicken Sandwich or
Grilled Lemon Honey Prawns over Brown Rice
Potato Salad
Broccoli Salad

Dessert
Red, White and Blue Strawberry/Blueberry Short Cake

Recipes

Jalapeño Corn Bread Poppers

Ingredients

1	cup corn meal
1	cup flour
3	tbsps. baking powder
1	tsp. salt
1	egg
1	cup buttermilk
¼	cup oil
¼	cup medium cheddar cheese
2	jalapeños seeded and chopped finely
1	cup of Panko bread crumbs

Directions

Fryer set to 375 degrees. Sift all dry ingredients into large mixing bowl and set aside. Beat the egg and then add milk and oil and mix well. Add the wet mixture to the dry and mix until well blended. Add cheese and jalapeños and mix in well. Use a cookie scoop to make dough into balls. Roll the balls in the Panko bread crumbs and place on parchment paper. Put 5 balls in the fryer and cook until they are dark golden brown and float. Serve hot or cooled. Great served with honey drizzled on top or just the poppers.

Cucumber and Onion

Ingredients

- 3 large cucumbers peeled and sliced to about ¼" thick
- 3 medium sweet onions peeled and sliced about ¼" thick
- 2 tsps. salt
- 2 tsps. pepper
- 1 cup apple cider vinegar
- 1 cup water

Directions

In a mixing bowl add all the ingredients and stir to mix up the water and vinegar. Cover and refrigerate. Best if left for a day or two before serving.

BBQ Inside Out Cheese Burgers or Ground Pork Burgers

Ingredients

2	lbs. ground beef (20% fat) or ground pork
8	cubes of medium cheddar cheese
1	tsp. salt
1	tsp. pepper
1	tsp. garlic powder

Directions

Mix the ground beef or pork, salt, pepper and garlic powder together completely. Then separate meat into 8 balls. Place one cube of cheese in each of the balls, covering the cheese completely with the meat and form into a patty. Grill the hamburgers to preferred doneness. Be sure to cook to appropriate temperature for beef (internal temp. of a minimum of 145 degrees). Get creative with your bun choices and toppings. One suggestion would be to have quite an array of condiments.

Spicy Chicken Sandwich

Ingredients

Boneless chicken breast (one for each sandwich)
Salt
Pepper
Garlic powder
Pickled jalapeño rounds
Beefsteak tomatoes (enough for all the sandwiches)
Lettuce (your choice)
Sweet onion (enough for all sandwiches)
Condiments (be creative and have many choices)
Kaiser rolls (enough for each sandwich)

Directions

Make sure your grill is well oiled. Salt, pepper and sprinkle garlic powder on each chicken breast before grilling. Let that sit while you prepare the other ingredients. Slice the tomato and onion fairly thin and place on a platter with the lettuce. Set out all of your condiments and rolls. Grill the chicken and be sure that it does not cook too quickly so that the inside temperature reaches 165 degrees without burning on the outside.

Grilled Lemon Honey Prawns Over Brown Rice

Ingredients

	Prawns (enough for guests)
⅓	cup of honey
2	lemons
	Salt
	Pepper
2	cups of cooked brown rice
	Fresh mint

Directions

Make sure the prawns are cleaned, washed and dried before you begin to work with them. While the prawns are drying, you may begin making the sauce that will be brushed on the prawns while they cook. In a bowl, add the honey, zest of one lemon, juice of one lemon, ½ tsp. of salt, and ¼ tsp. of pepper. Mix that together thoroughly and set aside. Chop your fresh mint for garnish. Once your brown rice has cooked (follow cooking instructions on the package), put it in a serving bowl and add the zest of the other lemon and the juice from the other lemon and mix with the rice. Keep your rice warm while you grill the prawns. Make sure your grill is well oiled. Use a pastry brush to brush the honey mixture on each side of the prawns while you grill. The prawns will cook quickly. They should be nice and pink. Usually 3-4 minutes on each side. Make sure that the cooking side as had the honey mixture brushed on it before cooking. Serve over the rice and garnish with the fresh mint.

Potato Salad

Ingredients

7	medium russet potatoes
8	large eggs hardboiled
1	large purple onion
1	16 oz. jar of sweet pickles
1	16 oz. jar of Miracle Whip
	Salt
	Pepper

Directions

Boil potatoes until thoroughly cooked (fork should slide right out of potato when poked). Set the potatoes aside to cool. Dice eggs and place in large mixing bowl. Dice purple onion and place with the eggs. Dice the sweet pickles and place with eggs. Once the potatoes are cooled, peel them. Then quarter each potato and cut each quarter into quarters. Place the potatoes with the other ingredients. Add the whole jar of Miracle Whip and mix well. If a little dry, add a tablespoon of the juice from the pickles. Salt and pepper the salad to taste. Cover and refrigerate at least 2 hours before serving.

Broccoli Salad

Ingredients

1	lb. of broccoli tops
1	lb. of bacon, fried and diced
¼	cup of finely chopped onions
1	cup of Miracle Whip
	Salt
	Pepper

Directions

Chop the broccoli tops and place in mixing bowl. Add the diced bacon and onions. Add the Miracle Whip and mix. Add salt and pepper to taste. Cover and refrigerate at least 2 hours before serving.

Red, White and Blue Strawberry/Blueberry Short Cake

Ingredients for Short Cake Biscuit

1	cup flour
1	tsp. baking powder
1	tsp. salt
¼	tsp. baking soda
6	tbsps. butter
1	cup milk
¼	cup sugar

Directions

Preheat the oven to 450 degrees. Cover cookie sheet with parchment paper. Sift together flour, baking powder, salt, and baking soda. Using a pastry cutter, mix in the butter until you get little balls. Add the milk and sugar and mix until you can form the dough into a ball. Add flour a little at a time, if you need it. Do not over work the dough. Use a spoon to scoop a bit of the biscuit dough out of the bowl and place on the parchment paper-covered cookie sheet. Cook for 7-8 minutes. Biscuit should be golden brown when it comes out of the oven. Let cool.

Ingredients for Strawberries

1	quart of strawberries washed, dried and sliced
1	cup of sugar

Directions for Strawberries

Mix the strawberries and sugar together and place in refrigerator until the biscuits are cooled completely.

Ingredients for the Whipped Cream

1	small basket of blueberries
1	16 oz. container of heavy whipping cream
¼	cup of confectioners' sugar
1	tsp. vanilla extract

Directions

Use a stand mixer and be sure the mixing bowl has been kept cold before using. Mix the container of whipping cream until it starts to form fluffy peaks. Add the confectioners' sugar and vanilla extract. Whip until you get nice stiff fluffy peaks. Be careful not to over whip it or it will turn to butter. Remove about a third of the whipped cream to use later. Now add the blueberries to the remaining whipped cream and mix by hand.

Directions for putting the shortcake together

Slice the biscuits in half. Place one half on a plate. Put a spoonful of the blueberry whipped cream on top of that half. Put the other half of the biscuit on top of that. Using the set aside whipped cream put a small amount on top. Now add a big spoonful of strawberries on top of that and serve.

Kathy during shoot cooking her Picnic Oven Fried Chicken.

August

Hot August nights and the lazy days of summer is an ideal time to enjoy lighter culinary fare while relaxing outdoors or inside with the doors wide open. And it's National Picnic Month - time to celebrate! Following are some menus the whole family can make while summer provides an opportunity join together without the stress of school and with lightened workloads, even perhaps making exciting preparations for a long-awaited vacation or putting together a favorite picnic basket. Have fun!

Picnic Basket Lunch (Meat)

Appetizers
Cantaloupe and Prosciutto

Entrée
Roast Beef Baguettes with Mustard Cream
and Arugula (keep the greens in a plastic bag for
freshness to add when you arrive at your destination,
if you are traveling to a park, etc.)
Kettle Chips
Cherry Tomato and Mozzarella Balls Salad

Dessert
Strawberry/Brownie Skewers
Lemon Iced Sweet Tea

Picnic Dinner (Poultry)

Appetizers
Hummus Dip

Pita Chips

Celery

Entrée
Picnic Oven-Fried Chicken Thighs and Drumsticks

Greek Potato Salad

Tomato cucumber salad with feta

Sourdough Bread

Dessert
Chocolate Chip Oatmeal Bars

Plums

Strawberry Lemonade

Outdoor Barbecue (Fish)

Appetizers
Eight-layer Dip
Tortilla Chips

Entrée
Shrimp and Chorizo Skewers
Corn Salad
Warm Tortillas with Lime Butter

Dessert
Watermelon, Cantaloupe and Feta Cheese Skewers

Recipes

Prosciutto and Melon

Ingredients

1   ripe cantaloupe seeded and cut into 8 wedges.
8   pieces thin prosciutto

Directions

Remove the flesh from the rind of the cantaloupe. Carefully wrap the prosciutto slices around each piece of melon.

Cover with plastic and keep cool as you journey to your picnic.

Roast Beef Baguettes

Ingredients

7	oz. thickened or heavy cream
¼	cup Dijon mustard
¾	cups Parmesan cheese
	Salt and pepper
2	tbsps. olive oil
1	small roast beef (about 2 lbs.)
2	sourdough baguettes
2	cups loosely packed arugula
2	jars of apple raisin chutney

Directions

Combine cream and mustard in a small saucepan over medium heat. Bring to just below simmer, add Parmesan, stir until melted. Season this to taste with salt and pepper and set aside to cool.

Preheat oven to 280 degrees F.

Heat olive oil in a large frying pan over high heat, season the beef fillet to taste and cook, turning occasionally, until browned (1-2 minutes each side). Transfer to an oven tray and roast in oven until cooked (25-30 minutes for medium rare) set aside to rest (30 minutes). Slice thinly. Halve the baguettes lengthways and spread bases with chutney. Top with roast beef and arugula, drizzle with mustard cream and season to taste. Wrap and put into your picnic basket.

Cherry Tomatoes and Mozzarella Ball Salad

Ingredients

- ¼ cup extra virgin olive oil
- ¼ cup fresh basil, chopped
- 1 lb. Ciliegine mozzarella (cherry-sized mozzarella balls)
- Kosher salt and freshly-ground black pepper to taste
- 1 pint cherry or grape tomatoes (about 2 cups)
- 3 tbsps. golden balsamic vinegar

Directions

In a medium bowl, combine the olive oil and basil. Add the mozzarella and season to taste with salt and pepper. Cover and let marinate for at least 30 minutes in the refrigerator.

Add tomatoes and vinegar to the mozzarella and toss to combine. Season this to taste with more salt and pepper, if you like. Place mixture in a plastic container and put in the refrigerator until ready to leave for your picnic. Bring toothpicks so everyone can spear the delicious tomatoes and cheese!

Strawberry Brownie Skewers

Ingredients

- 12 mini-skewers or 6 halved
- 24 strawberries, rinsed, ends removed
- 12 large marshmallows
- 12 two-bite brownie bites (store bought)
- ½ cup chocolate chips

Directions

Layer the skewers with a strawberry, a marshmallow, a brownie bite, and another strawberry. Lay the skewers on a wax paper-lined baking sheet. Melt chocolate chips in a microwave-safe dish for about 30 seconds. Stir. Melt for an additional 20- 30 seconds or until chocolate has totally melted. Stir to incorporate until the desired consistency is reached. Add melted chocolate to a Ziploc bag and cut a small hole in the corner of the bag. Drizzle melted chocolate on top of completed kabobs. Place kabobs in refrigerator until chocolate sets.

Hummus Dip

Ingredients

1	can (15 oz) garbanzo beans, drained, liquid reserved
1	tbsp. lemon juice
1	tbsp. olive oil
1	clove garlic, crushed
½	tsp. ground cumin
½	tsp. salt
2	drops of sesame oil or to taste

Directions

Blend garbanzo beans, lemon juice, olive oil, garlic, cumin, and salt and sesame oil in a food processor. Stream reserved garbanzo bean liquid into the mixture with the machine turned on until desired consistency. Drop sesame oil over the top.

Serve with pita chips and celery sticks.

Picnic Chicken Oven-Fried Thighs and Drumsticks

Ingredients

- 2 cups buttermilk, well shaken
- 4 large garlic cloves, lightly crushed, then peeled
- 8 chicken thighs and 8 chicken drumsticks (5 lbs. total), skin on
- Cooking oil spray
- 1½ cups plain dried bread crumbs
- 1 tsp. dried oregano
- 1 tsp. dried basil
- 1 tsp. dried marjoram
- 1½ tsps. Kosher salt
- ½ tsp. freshly-ground pepper

Directions

Combine buttermilk and garlic in large bowl. Add chicken pieces and turn to coat. Cover and refrigerate at least an hour and up to 12 hours.

Preheat oven to 400 degrees F with a rack placed in the upper third of the oven.

Line a large shallow baking sheet with foil and spray lightly with cooking oil. In a large bowl, combine bread crumbs, oregano, basil, marjoram, salt and pepper. Toss very well to blend.

When time has passed, drain chicken and discard the buttermilk. Dredge each piece of chicken in bread crumbs until coated, then place skin side on baking sheet. Spray pieces with cooking oil. Bake chicken until golden and cooked through, 35 - 45 minutes. Transfer to a wire rack to cool. The chicken may be served warm or cold.

Kathy's Picnic Oven fried chicken.

Greek Potato Salad

Ingredients

12	red potatoes
½	cup green onion, chopped
¼	cup olive oil
¼	cup red wine vinegar
1½	tsps. fresh lemon juice
1½	tsps. garlic powder
½	tsp. onion powder
½	tsp. sea salt
½	tsp. freshly-ground pepper
¼	tsp. dried oregano
¼	tsp. white sugar
¼	tsp. dried rosemary, crumbled

Directions

In a large Dutch oven, place the red potatoes and then cover with salted water. Bring to a boil. Reduce heat to medium-low and simmer until tender about 25-30 minutes. Drain and then chill in freezer until cold, about 25-30 minutes.

When potatoes are cold, slice them and put them into a large salad bowl. Toss the potatoes with the green onion, then whisk, in a small bowl, the olive oil, red wine vinegar, lemon juice, garlic powder, onion powder, salt, black pepper, oregano, sugar, and rosemary. Pour dressing over the potatoes and toss. Place the salad in refrigerator until time to join the rest of the culinary features of the picnic.

Tomato, Cucumber Salad with Feta

Ingredients

- 6 cups English or Persian cucumbers, coarsely chopped (about 2 lbs.)
- 2 large tomatoes, coarsely chopped
- 1 bunch scallions, chopped
- 1 cup assorted sliced olives
- 1 7 oz. package feta cheese, crumbled, divided
- ½ fresh mint leaves, coarsely shopped
- 6 tbsps. extra virgin olive oil
- ¼ cup fresh lemon juice
- Sea salt and freshly-ground pepper

Directions

In a large bowl, combine cucumbers, tomatoes, scallions, olives, half of feta and the mint. Whisk oil and lemon juice together in a small bowl. Season the dressing with salt and pepper. Refrigerate. When ready to serve, pour dressing over salad and toss to coat. Season the salad to taste with salt and pepper. Sprinkle remaining half of feta over the salad. When traveling to a picnic destination, keep dressing and salad separate until ready to serve. Then toss the salad with the dressing.

Chocolate Chip Oatmeal Bars

Ingredients

½	cup melted butter
½	cup white sugar
½	cup brown sugar
¼	tsp. baking powder
¼	tsp. baking soda
¼	tsp. salt
1	large egg, beaten
½	tsp. vanilla
¼	tsp. cinnamon
⅛	tsp. nutmeg
1	cup white flour
¾	cup semi-sweet chocolate chips
¾	cup uncooked rolled oats

Directions

Preheat oven to 350 degrees F.

Melt the butter in a large microwave safe bowl. Add the white and brown sugars and let cool. Add egg, baking soda, baking powder, salt, cinnamon, nutmeg and vanilla.

Add flour and mix. Then add the chocolate chips and oats and combine with the other ingredients. The dough will be stiff. Spread the dough evenly with a spatula in a greased 8x8-inch baking pan.

Place the pan on the middle rack in oven and bake for 25-30 minutes at 350 degrees. Let cool and then cut into bars. It makes 16 bars.

Strawberry Lemonade

Ingredients

4½	cups fresh strawberries, halved
4	lemons
½	cup or more sugar
	Water
	Ice

Directions

Place strawberries and 1 cup of water in a blender. Run the bender until strawberries are smooth and then strain using a fine mesh strainer. Juice the lemons. They should yield about 1 cup of juice.

Combine sugar and ½ cup of water in a small jar. Shake until sugar is completely dissolved.

In a 2-quart pitcher, add strawberry juice, lemon juice and ¾ of the sugar mixture. Fill the pitcher halfway with ice. Add 4-5 cups of cold water and stir.

Taste and add more of the sugar mixture, if desired. Serve ice cold.

Makes 8 cups.

8-Layer Dip

Ingredients

1	can (16 oz.) refried beans
2	tsp. fresh lime juice
	Kosher salt and freshly-ground pepper
½	cup sour cream
½	cup grated cheddar cheese (2 oz.)
1	can (4.5 oz.) chopped green chilies
2	plum tomatoes, seeded and chopped
1	avocado, halved, pitted, peeled and diced
1	cup romaine lettuce, shredded
2	scallions, chopped

Directions

Combine beans, lime juice and 2 tablespoons of water in a medium bowl. Season the beans with salt and pepper. Transfer to a serving dish. Top with sour cream, then cheese, chilies, tomatoes, avocado, lettuce and scallions. Refrigerate until ready to serve.

Serve with sturdy tortilla chips. Serves 4.

Shrimp and Chorizo Skewers

Ingredients

14	raw jumbo shrimp, peeled and deveined with the tails intact (about 2 lbs.)
1	garlic clove, minced
¼	cup extra virgin olive oil
2	tbsps. fresh lime juice
1	lime, cut into wedges
8	oz. chorizo sausage, links cut diagonally in sixteen 1-inch pieces
1	avocado, halved pitted, peeled and wedged
	Coarse salt
	Freshly-ground pepper
	Wooden skewers

Directions

Soak 8 wooden skewers in water to prepare them for the grill.

In a large baking dish, place shrimp, garlic, oil and lime juice. Toss well. Cover and marinate in the refrigerator for 30 minutes, turning occasionally.

Preheat grill to medium high.

Alternate 3 shrimp and 2 chorizo slices, starting with the shrimp, onto each skewer. Omit the sausage for those who do not eat meat. Season the skewer with salt.

Grill until shrimp are opaque and chorizo is slightly softened, about 3 minutes per side.

Arrange avocados on a platter. Squeeze lime wedges over avocado and season with salt and pepper. Serve with shrimp and chorizo skewers. Serves 4-6.

Corn Salad

Ingredients

3	cups raw corn kernels (from about 4 cobs of corn)
1	medium ripe tomato, chopped
¾	cup green onion, chopped
1	cucumber, quartered and thinly sliced
½	cup fresh leafy herbs (e.g., basil, dill, mint, parsley and/or cilantro) chopped
¼	cup extra virgin olive oil
1	tbsp. white wine vinegar
2	medium garlic cloves, minced
½	tsp. fine sea salt or pink Himalayan salt, to taste
	Freshly-ground pepper

Directions

Combine the corn, tomato, green onion, cucumber, herbs, and radishes in a large serving bowl.

Combine the olive oil, vinegar, garlic, salt and pepper in a small bowl. Whisk until blended. Pour dressing over the salad and toss. Taste and adjust seasonings. Cover and keep in the refrigerator until ready to serve. Serves 4.

Watermelon, Cantaloupe and Feta Cheese Skewers

Ingredients

1	12 oz. block of feta cheese
1	cantaloupe, seeded, peeled and cut into eight 1-inch cubes
¼	small seedless watermelon, peeled and cut into eight 1-inch cubes
3	tbsps. balsamic glaze
	Fresh basil leaves, for garnish
	Small skewers or long toothpicks

Directions

Cut feta cheese in 24 cubes, slightly smaller than the melon cubes.

Set 1 piece of feta cheese on top of each piece of cantaloupe and watermelon and secure with a toothpick. Place the skewers on a serving plate and drizzle the balsamic glaze over the top. Garnish with the basil leaves. Makes 24 bites.

Scot's Almond English Toffee

September

September was always the signal that summer is over and it's time to go back to school. But there was that one last weekend of summer fun. Labor Day weekend was the last hurrah of summer. Of course, I just knew that school was starting and didn't understand the holiday until I was an adult. But most of all, September for me is the start of fall and the wonderful flavors that come with this time of year. As the days get shorter and the nights colder, the meals get heartier.

This time of year is meant for stocking up. We would get the wood pile readied, meat in the freezer and the fireplace cleaned and ready for the new season.

Labor Day Beef, Chicken, Pork or Fish

Appetizer
Pork Fried Wontons with Dipping Sauce

First Course
Stuffed Mushrooms

Entrée
Sweet and Spicy Chicken, Beef, Pork or Fish
Rosemary Sage Steamed Rice
Carrot and Turnip Mash

Dessert
Chocolate Chip Cheesecake

Recipes

Fried Pork Wontons and Dipping Sauce

Ingredients for wontons

- 1 package of wonton wrappers
- ½ pound of pork sausage (mild or spicy, your choice)
- ¼ cup finely chopped onions

Ingredients for dipping sauce

- ¼ cup of sugar
- ¼ cup raspberries
- 1 tbsp. rice wine vinegar
- ½ tsp. mustard powder

Directions

Heat the fryer to 375 degrees. Cook the pork sausage in a saucepan over medium heat. Drain the fat. Place a spoonful of pork sausage in the center of the wonton wrapper and place a few of the finely chopped onions on top of the sausage. Use your finger or pastry brush to brush on a little water around the four edges of the wonton wrapper. Fold the wonton up by the corners and twist. Finish with all the wontons. Place them in the fryer 5 at a time. Cook until golden brown and floating to top. Remove them and place on paper towels to remove excess oil. Serve hot.

In a saucepan over medium heat, mix the ingredients. Cook until reduced to thick sauce. Cool and serve in dipping bowl with wontons.

Stuffed Mushrooms

Ingredients

1	quart button mushrooms
¼	onions
¼	red bell pepper
½	cup Monterey Jack cheese
	Olive oil

Directions

Preheat the oven to 400 degrees. Wash and dry the mushrooms and bell pepper. Remove the caps from the stem of the mushroom. Finely chop the stems and place them in a bowl. Finely chop your onion and bell pepper and add to the mushroom that you chopped. Add the Monterey Jack cheese and mix well. Using a pastry brush, brush olive oil all over the caps and place them in a parchment-covered cookie sheet. Using a teaspoon, fill each cap with the mixture you made. Bake the mushrooms for 15 minutes or until they are nice brown on top. Serve hot.

Sweet and Spicy Chicken, Beef, Pork or Fish

Ingredients

1	lb. boneless chicken thigh (replace both chicken with 1 pound of cubed ribeye, cubed pork shoulder, or a nice cubed white fish)
1	medium onion
1	pineapple
1	red pepper
1	yellow pepper
1	green pepper
⅓	cup of sesame oil
1	cup flour
1	tsp. salt
1	tsp. pepper
2	tsps. crushed red pepper
1	cup milk
2	eggs
½	cup sugar
½	cup honey
¼	cup of Sriracha sauce
3	tbsps. rice wine vinegar

Directions

Cube the meat. Mix the flour, salt, pepper and crushed red pepper. In another bowl mix the milk and eggs. Dredge the meat in the flour, then the egg mix and then back in flour. Be sure to get excess flour off the meat and place on parchment paper while waiting to fry. In a frying pan, place the sesame oil. Heat on high and once oil is hot, reduce heat to medium and fry the meat. Remove the meat to paper towel so that excess oil is removed. In a large saucepan add sugar, honey Sriracha and rice wine vinegar. Heat to medium and mix the ingredients. Cook until thick. You may raise the temperature of stove if it is not cooking. Remove from heat and set aside. Cut the peppers, onion, and pineapple into nice bite-sized chunks. Put the saucepan back on medium heat. Add the meat, peppers, onions and pineapple. Mix all the ingredients until they are coated and the entire dish is hot. Place in serving dish.

Sage and Rosemary Steamed Rice

Ingredients

2	cups of water
1	tbsp. butter
1	cup long-grained rice
¼	cup chopped fresh sage
¼	cup chopped fresh rosemary
2	tsps. salt
2	tsps. pepper

Directions

Bring the 2 cups of water to a boil. Add butter and salt to the boiling water. Once butter is melted, add the rice and stir completely. Once the rice begins to boil again, turn heat down and let simmer for 40 minutes. After the 40 minutes are done, remove it from the heat. With a fork, fluff the rice and the chopped sage and rosemary and mix well. Then add the pepper. Fluff rice again and move to serving dish.

Carrot and Turnip Mash

Ingredients

5	carrots
2	large turnips
1	stick of butter
	Salt
	Pepper
1	cup sour cream

Directions

Wash and peel the carrots and turnips. Cut the carrots into about 2-inch pieces and place in large boiling pot. Cut the turnips into quarters and place in the pot. Cover the vegetables to about an inch above with water. Boil until you can smash the carrots and turnips with a fork. Drain them completely. Add the stick of butter to the vegetables and using a hand masher, mash the vegetables and butter until fairly smooth. Add salt and pepper to taste. Finally add the cup of sour cream and mix using a spoon.

Chocolate Chip Cheesecake

Ingredients

1¾	cup graham crackers crushed in food processor
⅓	cup melted butter
1¼	cups sugar
2	8-ounce packages of cream cheese
1	8-ounce package of mascarpone cheese
1	cup sour cream
1	tsp. vanilla extract
3	eggs
1	12 oz. package of dark chocolate chips
1	12 oz. package of mini-chocolate chips

Directions

Preheat the oven to 350 degrees. Mix the graham crackers and butter and then press that to the bottom of a springform pan. Push the mixture up just a bit on the sides. Set this aside. In a mixing bowl, mix the cream cheese and mascarpone together until fluffy. Mix in the sugar, sour cream, and vanilla until well mixed. Finally add the eggs one at a time mixing each in completely. With a spoon, mix the dark chocolate chips into the batter. Make sure the chocolate chips are spread evenly throughout the batter. Pour the batter evenly over the graham cracker crust. Place the cake on a cookie sheet in case of spills. Place in the middle of the oven and bake for 1 hour to 1 hour and 10 minutes. The cake should not jiggle when moved and the color should be a nice soft golden brown. Remove from oven and let cool. Once the cake is cooled, you may remove it from the springform pan and place on serving dish. Decorate the top with whipped cream and the mini-chocolate chips. Chill until ready to serve.

Cissy enjoying a joke over a great Halloween holiday meal Mr. French made.

October

Spooks, Spirits, Ghosts and Goblins; these are things that go bump in the night! All of these eerie phenomena can be accompanied by wonderfully comforting dishes which make October and especially Halloween extra special. Mr. French even shared the kitchen with the kids and me to create ghoulish delights! The stuffed pumpkin recipe is one I make with my own family every year and they love it! Whether you have a party, create a family celebration or just make special treats to hand out to costumed revelers at your door, making treats can be just as much fun as eating them. Here are some treats for great Halloween fests with no tricks!

Halloween Night Dinner (Meat)

Appetizers
Goblin Cheese Ball

Entrée
Stuffed Pumpkin
Ghostly Garlic Bread
Green Salad with Mandarin Oranges and Olives

Dessert
Graveyard Pudding

Halloween Dinner (Poultry)

Appetizers
Pumpkin Soup

Crazy Croutons

Entrée
Chicken Bat Wings

Scalloped Potatoes with Smoked Gouda

Brainy Cauliflower

Dessert
Candy Corn Cupcakes

Hot Cider

Kathy's Pumpkin Soup.

Halloween Dinner (Vegetarian)

Appetizers
Spooky Snacks

Entrée
Pumpkin Cannelloni
Spinach, Cucumber and Carrot Salad
Garlic Breadstick Fingers

Dessert
Halloween Pumpkin Cake

Recipes

Goblin Cheese Ball

Ingredients

- 2 eight oz. packages cream cheese, softened
- 4 tbsps. butter, slightly softened
- 1 tbsp. milk
- 2 cups shredded combination of cheeses, e.g. cheddar, jack, etc.
- 2 eight oz. packages of whipped cream cheese
- 2 black tortilla chips
- 1 small, whole pepper, like chili pepper, jalapeno, pepperoni, etc.
- 2 pimento-stuffed green olives
- 1 small green pepper, cut into two thin strips and 6 small triangles
- 6 pitted green olives
- Handful of julienned carrots
- Handful of shredded purple cabbage
- Toothpicks
- Assorted crackers and raw vegetables

Directions

Put the softened cream cheese, butter, and milk in an electric mixing bowl. Beat until smooth and combined, scraping down the sides of the bowl. Add the shredded cheeses and mix until well combined. Cover with plastic and chill in the refrigerator for least 4 hours and up to 24 hours.

Remove the chilled cheese mixture from the refrigerator. Place the cheese ball onto a wax paper-lined serving dish and form a round head-like shape. Stir the whipped cream cheese until very smooth. Spread the cheese ball evenly with the whipped cream cheese.

Press tortilla chips on the ball on each side for the ears.

Skewer the pepper with a toothpick and attach to the center of the cheese ball for the nose.

Press the pimento-stuffed olive in the head for eyes. Use the two strips of green bell pepper to form the eyebrows. Take the bell pepper triangles and insert them into the pitted green olives. Once the olives are assembled press those into the bottom of the cheese ball to form toes. Press the carrot strings into the head to make teeth. Finally, press the cabbage into the top of the cheese head to make hair.

Serve with cracker and raw vegetables. Makes about 20 servings.

Stuffed Pumpkin

Ingredients

1	small whole sugar pumpkin, about 10 inches in diameter
2	tbsps. salad oil
2	lbs. ground beef (can use portobello mushrooms)
1	large onion, finely chopped
1	medium green pepper, finely chopped
2	tsps. salt
2	tsps. oregano
1	tsp. apple cider vinegar
	Freshly-ground pepper, to taste
2	cloves garlic, mashed
¾	cup seedless raisins
⅓	cup pimiento-stuffed green olives, sliced
2	tsps. capers
1	8-ounce can tomato sauce
½	cup red wine
3	eggs, beaten

Directions

Preheat oven to 350 degrees F. Wash pumpkin. Cut a 6-inch circle around stem. Remove the top and set aside. Discard seeds or save for toasting. Remove loose fibers from the interior of the pumpkin.

In a heavy skillet with a cover, heat the salad oil. Add ground beef, onion, and green pepper. Cook over medium-high heat until beef is browned and crumbly. Remove from heat and add salt, oregano, vinegar, pepper and garlic. Stir in raisins, olives, and capers, then gradually add tomato sauce and red wine. Cover skillet, return to heat and simmer for about 15 minutes, stirring occasionally. Cool slightly and add beaten eggs, mixing thoroughly.

Sprinkle the inside of the reserved pumpkin with a little salt, then fill with the meat stuffing, pressing to pack firmly. Cover loosely with pumpkin lid and place on a greased 15x10x1" baking pan. Rub oil on the outside of the pumpkin. Bake uncovered for about 1½ hours or until pumpkin is tender. Allow to cool for about 10-15 minutes before serving.

To serve, carefully lift stuffed pumpkin onto a serving plate. Slice through top to bottom in flat wedges, spooning more meat filling onto each slice. Serves 8.

Green Salad with Mandarin Oranges and Olives

Ingredients

1	can (15 oz.) Mandarin oranges in light syrup, drained
½	cup halved pitted Kalamata olives or sliced black olives
¼	cup extra virgin olive oil
1	tbsp. white vinegar
½	tsp. cumin, ground
¼	tsp. paprika
1	head of butter lettuce, torn into 1½-inch pieces
1½	tsps. flat-leaf Italian parsley, chopped
	Himalayan sea salt to taste
	Freshly-ground pepper to taste

Directions

Place drained oranges into a medium bowl. Add drained olives to same bowl.

In another bowl, whisk oil and next three ingredients to blend. Add to the orange

mixture. Toss to coat. Season the mixture with salt and pepper to taste.

Divide lettuce among 4 plates. Top the lettuce leaves with orange mixture. Sprinkle with parsley and refrigerate or serve.

Ghostly Garlic Bread

Ingredients

8	medium garlic cloves with skin left on
6	tbsps. unsalted butter, softened
2	tsps. Parmesan cheese, grated
½	tsp. sea salt
	Freshly-ground black pepper
2	demi baguettes
6	string cheese sticks
16	black olive slices

Directions

Preheat oven to 500 degrees F with oven rack on the lower third position.

Place garlic cloves in a small skillet. Cook over medium heat, shaking pan occasionally until the cloves are slightly browned. About 8 minutes. Cool.

Skin and then mince garlic cloves or press them through a garlic press. Mash the garlic, softened butter, Parmesan cheese, salt and a pinch of pepper with a fork until well combined.

Cut each of the small baguettes in half lengthwise and then again in half crosswise so you have eight halves. Spread the cut side of each of the halves with the prepared garlic butter.

Thinly peel apart the string cheese. Place two slices of black olives on each half for eyes and then the pieces of string cheese in layers on top of the bread halves to look like wrapped mummies. Pretty ghostly!

Transfer the halves buttered and cheese side up onto a baking sheet. Bake at 500 degrees for 6-8 minutes until the cheese is melted and just beginning to brown. Serve immediately. Serves 8.

Graveyard Pudding

Ingredients

2	packages (3.9 oz.) chocolate-flavor instant pudding
3	cups cold milk
1	tub (12 oz.) Cool Whip topping, thawed, divided
15	Oreo cookies, crushed (about 1 ½ cups)

Assorted decorations: 3 oblong vanilla crème-filled sandwich cookies, small decorating gel tube, 5 candy pumpkins.

Directions

Place pudding mixes and milk in a large bowl and beat with a whisk for two minutes. Let stand 5 minutes. Stir in 3 cups of Cool Whip and half the cookie crumbs. Spread into a 13x9-inch serving dish; sprinkle with remaining crumbs. Refrigerate 1 hour. Meanwhile, decorate sandwich cookies with decorating gel to resemble tombstones.

Just before serving, insert decorated cookie into top of dessert. Drop large spoonfuls of remaining Cool Whip on the dessert to resemble ghosts.

Pumpkin Soup

Ingredients

½	cup onion, finely chopped
2	tbsps. butter
1	tbsp. all-purpose flour
2	cans (14½ oz. each) chicken broth
1	can (15 oz. solid pack pumpkin)
1	tsp. brown sugar
½	tsp. salt
⅛	tsp. pepper
⅛	tsp. freshly-ground nutmeg
1	cup heavy whipping cream

Directions

In a large saucepan, sauté the onion in butter until it is tender. Remove from heat; stir in flour until smooth. Gradually stir in the broth, pumpkin, brown sugar, salt and pepper, and nutmeg. Bring to a boil. Reduce heat and simmer for five minutes. Add cream. Cook the soup for 2 minutes or until heated through. Place croutons on top and serve the soup. (Crouton recipe follows.) Serves 6.

Crazy Croutons

Ingredients

1	loaf French bread
3	tbsps. olive oil
3	tbsps. butter
	Garlic powder to taste

Directions

Slice the loaf of bread into ½-inch-thick slices, then cut the bread into cubes. Heat half of the olive oil in the skillet over medium heat and then add ½ of the butter to melt. Add half of the bread cubes and stir to coat. Cook the cubes and stir every minute or so until the cubes are brown and crispy.

Transfer the crisp croutons to a tray to cool. Add the second half of the oil, butter and cubes and repeat the process.

After cooling the croutons, use immediately or keep them in an airtight container for 1-2 weeks. Serves 8.

Chicken Bat Wings

Ingredients

4-5	lbs. whole chicken wings
1¼	cups teriyaki stir-marinade sauce
¼	honey
2	tbsps. onion seasoning
¼	tsp. cayenne pepper, if you want more spice

Directions

Place chicken wings in a gallon resealable freezer bag. In a small bowl, combine teriyaki marinade, honey, onion seasoning and, if using, cayenne pepper. Pour marinade into bag; seal. Toss to coat. Place bag in a shallow dish and refrigerate overnight. Toss 2-3 times while marinating.

Preheat oven to 425 degrees F. Line 2 large baking sheets with foil. Spray foil with cooking spray. Remove chicken wings from plastic bag. Discard marinade. Place in a single layer on baking sheets. Bake wings for 20-30 minutes. Serves 8-10.

Scalloped Potatoes with Gouda Cheese

Ingredients

3	lbs. red potatoes, skin on, sliced
7	oz. Gouda cheese, shredded and divided
¼	lb. butter
8-10	cloves of garlic, minced
1½	cups heavy cream
1	tsp. salt
½	tsp. pepper

Directions

Preheat oven to 325 degrees F. Butter a 9x13" baking dish. Melt the butter in a small pan and sauté garlic until nicely browned. Layer half of the thinly sliced potatoes in the bottom of the baking pan. Sprinkle half of the Gouda cheese on top. Top with the other half of the sliced potatoes. Pour on the butter-garlic mixture.

Combine the heavy cream with the salt and pepper and pour on top of the potatoes. Sprinkle the rest of the Gouda cheese on top. Bake for 75 minutes. Serve immediately.

Brainy Cauliflower

Ingredients

1	cauliflower, whole
¼	cup olive oil
½	cup white wine
	Salt and pepper to taste
¼	cup tomato sauce
¼	cup Thousand Island dressing

Directions

Cut the stems from the cauliflower and steam for about 30 minutes.

Remove to a serving platter. Spoon the dressing over the cauliflower. Drip tomato sauce over to look like veins on the brainy cauliflower.

Candy Corn Cupcakes

Ingredients

1	cup whole milk, room temperature
6	large eggs, whites only, room temperature
2	tsps. almond extract
1	tsp. vanilla extract
2¼	cups cake flour
1¾	cups sugar
4	tsps. baking powder
1	tsp. salt
1½	sticks unsalted butter (2 tbsps.), cut into 12 pieces and softened

For the frosting

3	sticks unsalted butter, cut into chunks and softened
3	tbsps. heavy cream
2½	tsps. vanilla extract
¼	tsp. salt
3	cups confectioners' sugar
24	candy corn candies

Directions

For the cupcakes

Place the oven racks on the upper middle and lower middle position in the oven.

Preheat oven to 350 degrees F.

Line two 12-cup muffin tins with cupcake liners to fit.

In a small bowl, whisk together the milk, egg whites, and extracts.

In a large bowl, whisk together the flour, sugar, baking powder and salt.

With an electric mixer set on medium-low speed, beat the butter, one piece at a time, into the flour mixture, about 30 seconds. Continue to beat the mixture until it resembles moist crumbs, about 1-2 minutes.

Beat in all but ½ cup of the milk mixture, then increase the mixer speed to medium and beat the batter until smooth, light and fluffy, 1-3 minutes. Reduce the mixer speed to low and slowly beat in the remaining ½ cup of the milk mixture, about 15 seconds.

Lightly grease a ¼ cup measuring cup to pour the batter evenly into the cupcake liners.

Bake the cupcakes, switching and rotating the pans halfway through the baking for a total of 15-20 minutes. Test for doneness with a light finger touch.

Let the cupcakes cool in the tins for 10 minutes and then transfer them to a wire rack to cool completely.

For the frosting

Beat the butter, cream, vanilla, and salt together in a large bowl with an electric mixer on medium-high speed until smooth, 1-2 minutes. Reduce the mixer speed to medium-low and slowly add the confectioners' sugar and beat until smooth, 4-6 minutes. Increase the mixer speed to medium-high and beat until the frosting is light and fluffy, 5-10 minutes.

Divide the frosting into three bowls and tint one yellow, one orange and leave one white.

Using a pastry bag or a plastic bag with the corner removed, pipe the frosting in a cone shape on the cupcake to resemble a candy corn.

Top each cupcake with a candy corn candy. Makes 24 cupcakes.

Spooky Snacks

Ingredients

2	large red peppers
2	large orange peppers
	Package of pre-cut celery sticks
	Package of baby carrots
	Pre-made ranch dressing of your choice

Directions

Wash peppers and cut off tops. Remove stem membrane from interior of peppers.

Carve out jack-o'-lantern faces on each of the peppers. Fill orange peppers with celery and red peppers with carrots.

Place on a serving dish with the ranch dressing in a small dipping bowl.

Pumpkin Cannelloni

Ingredients

1½	lb. pumpkin
1½	tbsps. extra virgin olive oil
3	large garlic cloves
½	cup ricotta cheese
½	cup Parmigiano-Reggiano cheese, grated
1½	tsps. fresh sage, finely chopped
¼	tsp. salt
½	tsp. pepper, freshly ground
1	package oven-ready lasagna sheets
6	tbsps. unsalted butter

Directions

Preheat the oven to 350 degrees F.

Peel and seed the pumpkin, chop into bits and cook until soft. Remove to a medium bowl and mash pumpkin until smooth.

Heat 1½ tbsps. olive oil in a small skillet and sauté garlic until golden. Transfer garlic to a mortar pestle, and then crush into a paste. Stir cheese, chopped sage, salt and pepper and garlic paste into mashed pumpkin. Set aside.

Bring a large pot of water to boil. Cook lasagna sheets until tender, about 2 minutes. Transfer to a plate and drizzle with olive oil to prevent pasta from sticking together. Reserve ¼ cup pasta water for later.

Brush a medium baking dish liberally with oil. Place a lasagna sheet on a clean work space. Add 4 tablespoons of pumpkin mixture to the center of lasagna; roll into a cannelloni-shaped tube, and then transfer to prepared baking dish. Repeat with the remaining sheets.

Pour reserved pasta water over lasagna and cover tightly with foil. Bake until heated through and pasta is tender 20-25 minutes. Cook butter and sage leaves in small skillet over medium-high heat until golden brown. Drizzle over pumpkin cannelloni and serve immediately. Serves 6.

Cucumber Spinach and Carrot Salad

Ingredients

4-5	oz. spinach, rinsed and dried
2	small cucumbers or ½ English cucumbers
1	cup cherry tomatoes, halved
1	medium carrot, thinly sliced
¼	cup sliced almonds
1	tbsp. balsamic vinegar
2	tbsps. extra virgin olive oil
½	tsp. fresh dill
½	tsp. salt
¼	tsp. pepper

Directions

Rinse and dry the spinach. Transfer to a large salad bowl.

Slice the cucumbers, thinly slice the carrots and halve the cherry tomatoes. Toss all the vegetables into the salad.

In a small bowl, combine the dressing ingredients: 2 tbsps. vinegar, 2 tbsps. olive oil, ½ tsp. salt and ¼ tsp. pepper and dill. Briskly whisk the dressing ingredients together.

Sprinkle the top of the salad with sliced almonds and drizzle with balsamic vinegar. Serves 4.

Garlic Breadstick Fingers

Ingredients

¼ cup water

8 drops green food coloring

8 whole almonds

¼ stick butter, melted

    Garlic salt

    Parmesan cheese

Directions

Preheat the oven to 450 degrees F. Line a baking sheet with parchment paper or spray the pan with cooking spray.

Unroll dough and cut into ½-inch rectangular slices.

Mix water and food coloring in a small bowl. Brush on the pizza slices. Place on the prepared baking sheet.

Press an almond into pizza dough to serve as the "nail" for each breadstick finger. Brush the breadstick with butter, sprinkle with garlic salt and Parmesan cheese. Bake for 8-10 minutes or until golden brown. Makes 8 breadsticks.

Bootiful Pumpkin Cake

Make two recipes of this cake to make your Bootiful pumpkin

Ingredients

4	eggs, beaten
2	cups sugar
1	cup vegetable oil
1	can (15 oz.) can pumpkin
2	cups all-purpose flour
1	tsp. salt
2	tsps. baking soda
1½	tsps. cinnamon
1	sugar ice cream cone

Frosting

8	oz. package cream cheese, softened
¼	cup butter softened
1	tsp. vanilla extract

1½-2 cups powdered sugar

2-3   tbsps. milk

Directions

Preheat the oven to 350 degrees F.

Combine eggs, sugar and oil in a large bowl or the bowl of your electric mixer. Beat with mixer on high speed until batter is lemon-colored and thick. Blend in pumpkin; set aside.

In another bowl, whisk together flour, salt, baking soda and cinnamon. Add ½ cup at a time to the pumpkin mixture, beating well after each addition. Pour batter into a lightly greased Bundt pan. Bake for 30 minutes at 350 degrees then reduce temperature to 325 degrees and bake for an additional 20-25 minutes or until done. Cool completely before frosting.

With the two cakes made, invert one on top of the other. Prepare cream cheese frosting, reserving ½ cup for stem of pumpkin. Tint frosting with orange food coloring. Drizzle over cakes. Tint remaining frosting green. Frost the ice cream cone with green frosting and invert on top for the stem.

Scot's olive dip.

November

THE HOLIDAYS ARE UPON us! I have always loved the Holiday Season. Thanksgiving being the first! This was truly the time for family to gather and enjoy a huge scrumptious meal together with plenty of appetizers and desserts. But for me, it was all about watching the Macy's Thanksgiving Day Parade and seeing Santa at the very end. That meant that Christmas was on its way. Thanksgiving was usually spent at our house with our family. My dad would usually make the appetizers and my mother would make a large meal. Family usually brought a plethora of desserts to be enjoyed not just Thanksgiving Day, but the entire weekend. We would definitely eat our way through the holiday! Here are a few of my favorites!

Thanksgiving Day
Beef, Chicken, Pork or Fish

Appetizer
Olive Spread/Dip

First Course
Roasted Garlic Butter Baguette with Bacon and Provolone

Entrée
Honey and Clove Baked Ham; Rosemary, Orange and Lemon Stuffed Turkey; Stuffed Pork Roast; or Lemon Lime Panko-Crusted Halibut

Garlic Mashed Potatoes

Pecan Yams

Giblet Dressing/Stuffing

Lemon Green Beans

Dessert
Almond Chocolate Toffee

Recipes

Olive Spread/Dip

Ingredients

1	can of small black olives
1	small jar of green olives
1	small onion
1	garlic clove
¼	cup of chives
1	cup of sour cream
1	8-ounce package of sour cream
1	tsp. salt
1	tsp. pepper

Directions

In a food processor, add the black olives, green olives, the onion, the garlic clove and chives. This should all be chopped finely and placed into a mixing bowl. Add the remainder of the ingredients and mix well. Cover and chill until ready to serve. Serve with crackers, chips, pita chips or cut sourdough bread.

Roasted Garlic Butter Baguette with Bacon and Provolone

Ingredients:

1	baguette
1	bulb of garlic
1	stick of butter softened
¼	lb. of provolone cheese
½	lb. of cooked bacon

Directions

For roasted garlic, preheat oven to 350 degrees. Cut off the top of the bulb of garlic and place the garlic on a piece of foil. Place the garlic in the oven and cook for at least 1 hour. It is done when the garlic is caramelized. Remove and let cool.

To make the butter, remove all the pieces of garlic and place in a bowl. Use a fork to mash up the garlic. Place the stick of softened butter in with the garlic and mix until well blended. Let this sit for about an hour.

To make the baguette, cut the baguette into slices. Preheat the oven to 425 degrees. Spread the garlic butter onto each piece of sliced baguette and place on a parchment-lined cookie sheet. Your cooked bacon should be sitting on paper towels to soak excess grease. Cut bacon into pieces. Cover the baguette slices with bacon. Slice the provolone thinly and into pieces that will fit over the bacon. Place the cookie sheet into the oven and cook for 7 minutes or until the cheese is completely melted and a nice golden color. Serve hot.

Honey and Clove Baked Ham
(size of ham determines amount served)

Ingredients:
1   boneless ham (your choice of size and what kind but should not be sliced)
1   cup honey
1   cup firmly packed brown sugar
2   tbsps. brown mustard
     Whole cloves

Directions

Preheat the oven to 375 degrees. In a bowl, mix honey, brown mustard and brown sugar and set aside. Take the whole cloves and insert them around the entire ham (about 2 inches apart). Place the ham in a baking pan. With a pastry brush, brush the honey mustard brown sugar mix over the ham. Cover the ham and place in the middle of the oven. Cook the ham for 15 minutes per pound and be sure the internal temperature reaches at least 140 degrees. You can brush on the honey mustard brown sugar mixture about every 45 minutes while you cook the ham. The cover to the ham should loosely cover it. Remove the ham when done and let sit for 10 minutes before carving.

Rosemary, Lemon and Orange Stuffed Turkey

Ingredients:

1	turkey (size dependent on how many you need to serve. Be sure it is thawed completely before cooking and that you removed the giblets from inside the turkey)
4	oranges
4	lemons
6	fresh rosemary sprigs
	Salt
1	stick of butter

Directions

Preheat the oven to 325 degrees. Remove the neck and giblets and set aside. Rinse and dry the turkey. Generously salt the inside of the turkey and set aside. Cut your oranges and lemons in half and remove any seeds (a 14-pound turkey can hold 3 whole oranges and 3 whole lemons) and set aside. Take the stick of butter and rub it all over the outside and inside of the turkey. Take half an orange and rub it all over the outside of the turkey. Take half a lemon and rub it all over the outside of the turkey. Take 2 sprigs of rosemary and tie them together. Make 3 of those. Put one of the tied rosemary sprigs all the way inside the turkey. Start placing lemons and oranges in the turkey. At about half full, add another tied sprig of rosemary. Finish filling turkey and just before the end add the last sprig of rosemary and cover with an orange half and a lemon half. Cover and place in the oven. You will cook it for 20 minutes a pound. The last 20 minutes you will remove the cover so the turkey can brown. The internal temperature should be at least 165 degrees. Let the turkey sit for at least 10 minutes before carving.

Stuffed Pork Roast

Ingredients:

	Pork roast (size depends on your needs. For this recipe it would be a 4 lb. roast)
1	cup of dried bread, cubed
½	cup shredded Monterey Jack cheese
1	stick of butter
2	eggs
2	garlic cloves
1	tsp. sage
1	tsp. thyme
1	tsp. cayenne pepper
	Salt
	Pepper

Directions

Preheat your oven to 325 degrees. You are going to butterfly your pork roast. This means you are cutting it in half but not going all the way through; you can open the roast and it will look sort of like a butterfly and you can put your stuffing inside. In a mixing bowl, add all the dry ingredients and mix well with your hands. In a pan, melt the butter. While that is melting, beat two eggs in small bowl. Once the butter is melted, pour that over the dry ingredients and mix well. Add your eggs and cheese and mix well. Now place the stuffing evenly over the roast. Now roll the roast up and tie it together with butcher string. Three places along the roll should be enough to hold it together. Place the rolled roast in a baking pan and cook for 25 minutes per pound or until the internal temperature is at 160 degrees. Let it rest for at least ten minutes before slicing and serving.

Lemon Lime Panko-Crusted Halibut

Ingredients:

    Halibut (enough for guests)
- 3 lemons
- 3 limes
- 1 cup of Panko bread crumbs
- 2 tsps. salt
- 2 tsps. pepper

Directions

Preheat the oven to 400 degrees. Set halibut out on waxed paper. Make sure you have enough parchment-lined cookie sheets for your fish. In a mixing bowl, squeeze the juice of your lemons and limes and whisk together. With a pastry brush, brush the juice on all sides of the fish. In shallow pan, mix the Panko crumbs with the salt and pepper. Dredge your fish through the Panko crumbs, being sure that all sides are completely coated and place on the parchment-covered cookie sheets. Place the fish on the center rack and cook at the 400-degree temperature for 12 to 15 minutes until the Panko crust is golden brown and the fish is flaky (easy to test by using a fork). Let them rest for a couple of minutes before serving.

Garlic Mashed Potatoes

Ingredients:

8	medium potatoes
1	stick of butter
1	bulb of garlic
½	cup heavy cream
½	cup sour cream
2	tsps. salt
1	tsp. pepper

Directions

Preheat the oven to 425 degrees. Cut the top off a bulb of garlic. Place the bulb of garlic on small baking pan and place in oven and bake for 40 minutes. The garlic should be caramelized. Remove each clove and place in a small bowl and set aside. Peel and dice the potatoes. Fill a pot for boiling the potatoes. Bring the potatoes to a boil over high heat. Once the potatoes are boiling, turn heat down to medium and continue to boil them. They are done when they will not stick to a fork. Drain the potatoes and place the potatoes in large mixing bowl. Mix the potatoes with the stick of butter. Once the butter is mixed in, add the salt, pepper and the garlic you cooked earlier. Mix thoroughly. Add the sour cream and mix. Slowly add the cream, mixing a little at a time. If your potatoes are fluffy before all the cream is added, then don't add all. If your potatoes are not fluffy after you added the cream, add a little more until you get fluffy mashed potatoes.

Pecan Yams

Ingredients:

5	medium-sized yams
1	cup sugar
2	tsps. cinnamon
1	tsp. nutmeg
1	cup heavy cream
3	eggs (room temperature)
1	stick butter
1	tsp. salt
1	cup brown sugar
1	cup chopped pecans

Directions

Preheat the oven to 375 degrees. Fill a large boiling pot with water and place the yams inside. Be sure that all the yams are covered with water. Place on high heat until they begin to boil. Lower heat so the water is still boiling, but not roaring boil. Cook until you stab with fork and yam falls off fork without help. Drain and let the yams cool. Once the yams are cooled, peel them and place in large mixing bowl. Add the salt and butter to the yams. Using a hand masher, mash the yams, butter and salt together. Once it looks smooth, continue to next step. Add the sugar, cinnamon, nutmeg and heavy cream. Mix this well. Pour the mixture into a 9x13" pan. In a small bowl, mix the brown sugar and pecan together. Pour that mixture over the top of the yams. Bake in the middle of the oven for 45 minutes. Remove and let set for 10 minutes before serving.

Giblet Dressing/Stuffing

Ingredients:

1	large bag of cubed dried bread
2	eggs
4	celery stalks
1	medium sweet onion
1½	tsps. salt
1½	tsps. pepper
1	tsp. dried sage
	Cooked giblets
	Stalk from the giblets

Directions

Preheat the oven to 375 degrees. Take the giblets and neck from your turkey. Fill a large boiling pot and add your giblets and neck. Bring them to a boil. Add a pinch of salt and let simmer for about 2 hours. Remove from heat and let cool. Save the stock. Cut the giblets up and place in a large mixing bowl. Remove the meat from the neck and add to the large mixing bowl. Chop the celery into nice bite-sized pieces and add them to the mixing bowl. Chop the onion and add to the mixing bowl. Add the bread, eggs, salt, pepper, and sage to the mixing bowl. Mix it up really well. Add the stalk from the giblets and mix. The mixture should be very wet. Pour into a 9x13" pan. Bake for 40-45 minutes. Make sure it is cooked through. The dressing should be moist throughout with the top being golden brown. You could also use this mixture to stuff your turkey, just be sure your turkey gets to the internal temperature it is supposed to have when fully cooked.

Lemon Green Beans

Ingredients:
1	lb. fresh green beans
	Juice and zest from 2 lemons
1	stick of butter
	Salt
	Pepper

Directions

Blanch the green beans and place on paper towel to dry. While they are drying, put your lemon juice and butter in a saucepan and let the butter melt. Whisk the lemon and butter for about 30 seconds. Remove from heat and let set for about 10 minutes. Take a frying pan and pour the butter lemon mixture in and turn the burner to high. Once it begins to boil, place the green beans in and with tongs, stir the green beans and heat them up. It is okay if they get a little char on them. Test one by eating. If it bites through easily with a bit of a crunch, they are ready. This will usually take about 5 minutes. Drain the lemon butter mixture and place the green beans on serving dish.

Almond English Toffee

Ingredients:

1	cup butter
1	cup sugar
¼	cup water
½	tsp. salt
½	cup chocolate chips
2	tbsps. heavy cream
1	cup chopped almonds

Directions

In a heavy saucepan, combine butter, sugar, water and salt. Cook to the hard-crack candy stage, 300 degrees. Stir constantly and watch carefully. Do not let it get too hot or remove before 300 degrees. Candy is finicky. If there is a lot of humidity in your cooking space, it could affect the outcome. Once it has reached the 300 degrees, immediately pour it into an ungreased 9x13" pan. Cool until hard. Using a double boiler melt the chocolate chips and heavy cream together. Once melted, pour over the toffee. Immediately sprinkle the chopped almonds over the chocolate. Press down on the almonds so they stick into the chocolate. Once the chocolate sets, you can break up the toffee and place on a serving dish.

Scot and Kathy ready to try her delicious Rum Cake.

December

December, the most festive month of all with Christmas, Hanukah and Kwanza. The Bill Davis family embraced Christmas heartily as revealed in one of its most popular episodes, "Christmas Came a Little Early," which demonstrated how important it is to love one another and our families throughout the year.

Christmas wreaths, fragrant pine trees and wonderful odors wafting throughout the house increase our pleasure of the holidays. Always nice to have some cinnamon sticks simmering in water on the stove or a candle pulsing the air with scents of balsam, cedar or cinnamon. Following are some of my favorite recipes - some my "real" family has enjoyed for years - I hope you do too!

Christmas Dinner (Meat)

Appetizers
Spiced Nuts

First Course
Fresh Crab with Remoulade Sauce

Entrée
Prime Rib Roast Beef with Horseradish Sauce

Popovers

Tomato Cups with Broccoli

Red Roasted Potatoes with Rosemary and Sage

Dessert
Rum Cake

Christmas Dinner (Poultry)

Appetizers
Caviar Pie

First course
Roquefort Pear Salad

Entrée
Roast Turkey
Savory Cornbread Dressing
Smashed Potatoes with Gravy
Brussels Sprouts with Bacon
Creamed Onions
Biscuits with Honey Butter

Dessert
Vanilla Bean Ice Cream with Hot Caramel Sauce
Christmas Cookies

Christmas Dinner (Fish)

Appetizers
Baked Brie with Cranberry Chutney

First course
Lobster Bisque

Entrée
Sole Almandine
Zucchini with Tomatoes
Christmas Rice
Hot Sourdough Bread

Dessert
Pecan Pie with Whipped Cream

Recipes

Spiced Nuts

Ingredients

- ¼ cup of packed brown sugar
- ½ tsp. ground cinnamon
- ¼ tsp. cayenne pepper
- 1 egg white
- 1 cup salted cashews
- 1 cup pecan halves
- 1 cup dry roasted peanuts
- ½ cup dried cranberries (optional)

Directions

Preheat the oven to 300 degrees F.

Combine the brown sugar, cinnamon, and cayenne in a small bowl. Set aside.

Whisk egg white in a large bowl; add nuts and, if using, cranberries. Sprinkle the nut mixture with the sugar mixture and toss to coat. Spread in a single layer on a greased baking sheet or a baking sheet lined with parchment paper.

Bake at 300 degrees for 18-20 minutes or until golden brown, stirring once halfway through the process. Cool. Store the nuts in an airtight container. Makes 3½ cups.

Fresh Crab Claws with Remoulade Sauce

Ingredients
Cold, cooked fresh crab claws for 6

Remoulade Sauce
- 1 cup mayonnaise
- 2 tbsps. fresh lemon juice
- 2 tbsps. Dijon mustard
- ¼ cup capers, coarsely chopped
- 2 tbsps. cornichon pickles, coarsely chopped (about 4)
- ¼ cup fresh parsley, coarsely chopped

Directions
Crack the claws and set aside.

Combine all ingredients for the remoulade sauce in a medium bowl. Refrigerate for at least an hour.

Put the sauce in small glass or ceramic containers with a sprinkle of chopped parsley on top of each. Place alongside the cracked crab on small plates and serve. Serves 6.

Prime Rib Roast Beef with Horseradish Sauce

Ingredients

1	(4-5) bone-in beef prime rib roast
1	bottle (750 ml) red wine
2	cups beef broth
2	tbsps. olive oil
2	tbsps. garlic
2	tbsps. fresh rosemary, minced
2	tbsps. fresh thyme, minced
1	tbsp. kosher salt
1	tsp. freshly-ground pepper

Horseradish Sauce

½	cup sour cream
2	tbsps. prepared creamed horseradish
1	tbsp. lemon juice
	Salt to taste

Directions

Have roast sit at room temperature for at least an hour before cooking.

Preheat oven to 450 degrees F. Place rack low enough so the roasting pan will sit in the middle of the oven.

Place a rack into the roasting pan. Add 2 cups of wine and the beef broth to the pan. Reserve the remaining wine. Set the roast in the rack, rib side down and fat side up. Mix olive oil, herbs, salad and pepper in a small bowl and spread over top of the roast.

Insert meat thermometer into meaty part of the roast, avoiding contact with the bones.

Roast for 20 minutes, then reduce heat to 350 degrees and continue cooking until the internal temperature reaches 115-120 degrees for medium rare (125-130 degree after

resting), 125-130 degrees for medium (135-140 degrees after resting).

Once removed from oven, transfer roast to platter and loosely tent with foil to allow to rest at least 15-20 minutes.

While the roast is resting, place the roasting pan on the burner with the rack removed. Add remaining wine and cook on low temperature to burn off some of the alcohol and work in the entire flavor from the bits left in the pan. Place warm sauce in a serving cup alongside the roast.

Serve with horseradish sauce.

Horseradish Sauce
In a small bowl, mix together all ingredients. Cover and refrigerate until ready to serve. Serves 6-8.

Popovers

Ingredients

5 tbsps. butter, melted

2 eggs

1 cup milk

1 tsp. sugar

1 tsp. salt

1 cup all-purpose flour

1 tsp. fresh thyme stems removed

Directions

Preheat oven to 425 degrees F. Drizzle a teaspoon or so of melted butter in each cup of a 12-cup muffin pan or a popover tin and place the baking pan in the oven while you make the batter.

Beat together the eggs, milk, 1 tablespoon of butter, the sugar and the salt. Beat in the flour a little bit at a time and add thyme. Mixture should be very smooth.

With pot holders, remove the muffin tin from the oven and fill each cup about halfway. Bake for 15-20 minutes, then reduce heat to 350 degrees and continue baking for 10 minutes more or until popovers are puffed and browned. Try not to peek, but let the popovers rise undisturbed.

Remove from pan and serve hot. Makes 12.

Tomato Cups with Broccoli

Ingredients

2	cups chopped broccoli
1	cup shredded cheddar cheese
¾	cup mayonnaise
	Salt to taste
	Freshly-ground pepper to taste
6-8	medium-sized tomatoes
1½	cup soft bread crumbs divided
1	cup grated Parmesan cheese

Directions

Preheat oven to 375 degrees F. Spray an 11x7x2" baking dish with cooking spray.

Combine ½ cup of the bread crumbs and ¼ cup of Parmesan cheese in a medium bowl. Set aside.

Cut a thin slice off the top of each tomato. Scoop out the pulp and place in a strainer over a bowl to drain. Place the tomato shells upside down on paper towels to drain.

Steam the broccoli until crisp tender. Chop tomato pulp and place in a large bowl. Add broccoli, cheddar cheese, mayonnaise, salt, pepper and remaining bread crumbs and Parmesan cheese. Mix gently. Stuff the tomatoes. Place the tomato cups on the baking pan. Sprinkle with reserved crumb mixture. Bake uncovered at 375 degrees for 30-40 minutes. Serves 6-8.

Red Roasted Potatoes with Rosemary and Sage

Ingredients

3	lbs. small red potatoes, scrubbed and quartered
¼	cup extra virgin olive oil
6	cloves of garlic, minced
3	tbsps. fresh rosemary leaves, chopped
4	medium sprigs fresh sage
	Kosher salt and pepper

Directions

Preheat the oven to 425 degrees F. Position a rack in the middle of the oven.

In a large bowl, combine potatoes, garlic, rosemary, and sage. Toss with the olive oil. Sprinkle on salt and pepper. Spread on a shallow rimmed baking sheet in one layer. Roast for about 45 minutes, stirring occasionally until the potatoes are tender.

Season with a little more salt and pepper and serve. Serves 6.

Rum Cake

(Everybody in my family loves this traditional cake for dinner, breakfast or anytime!)

Ingredients

Cake

1	cup chopped pecans or walnuts, or a combination of both
1	package yellow cake mix without pudding (18½ oz.)
1	package vanilla instant pudding (3¾ oz.)
4	large size eggs
½	cup cold water
½	cup vegetable oil
½	cup dark rum, Bacardi or Meyers (80 proof) (this recipe may not be for children)

Glaze

¼	lb. (½ cup) butter, sliced to melt faster
¼	cup cold water
1	cup granulated sugar
½	cup dark rum, Bacardi or Meyers (80 proof)

Directions

Preheat the oven to 325 degrees F. Grease with cooking spray and flour a ten- twelve-inch Bundt pan. Shake off excess flour. Sprinkle nuts evenly over the bottom of the prepared pan. Stir the dry ingredients together in a bowl. Add eggs, water, and oil. Turn up the speed on the mixer or the speed of your mixing! Pour prepared batter evenly over the nuts in the pan. Place on the middle rack of the oven and bake for 55 minutes.

When a tester comes out smooth or the top springs back lightly when touched remove the cake from the oven and let cool for at least ten minutes. Invert on a serving plate or cake platter. Prick the top, sides with a wooden or metal wooden skewer or fork.

For Glaze

Melt butter in a small saucepan over low heat. Stir in water and sugar. Boil for five minutes. Remove from heat. Then slowly stir in the rum.

Drizzle glaze over the cake. Use a baster, spoon and/or brush to redeem the excess glaze and place over the top of the cake, sides and interior. Enjoy!

Caviar Pie

Ingredients

4	hardboiled eggs, peeled and chopped
2	tbsps. mayonnaise
¾	cup sweet red onion, minced
6	oz. cream cheese, softened
½	cup sour cream
¼	cup chives, chopped

Directions

Spread onion on paper towel and drain about 30 minutes.

Lightly butter bottom and sides of an 8-inch springform pan. Stir together the chopped eggs and mayonnaise. Evenly spread into bottom of prepared pan. Sprinkle drained onion on top of egg mixture. Beat cream cheese and sour cream together until smooth. Drop by tablespoons onto the onion layer. Gently spread and smooth with the back of a spoon. Cover and chill for at least 3 hours or overnight. Once chilled, gently rinse caviar separately with cold water, drain in strainer, then on paper towel. Spoon the caviar on top of the cheese layer. Garnish with chives.

Serve with dark cocktail rounds. Serves 8-10.

Roquefort Pear Salad

Ingredients

1	package baby lettuce
3	pears, peeled, cored and chopped
5	oz. Roquefort cheese, crumbled
1	avocado, peeled, pitted and diced
½	cup green onion, thinly sliced
¼	cup glazed pecans
¼	cup dried cranberries
⅓	cup extra virgin olive oil
3	tbsps. balsamic vinegar
1	tsp. sugar
1	tsp. Dijon mustard
1	garlic clove, minced
½	tsp. salt
	Freshly-ground pepper to taste

Directions

Whisk together oil, vinegar, sugar, mustard, minced garlic, salt, and pepper. Layer lettuce, pears, Roquefort cheese, avocado and green onion in a large serving bowl. Pour dressing over salad, and top with pecans and cranberries. Serves 6.

Roast Turkey

Ingredients

1	fresh or totally defrosted turkey (10-12 lbs.)
¼	pound butter
1	tsp. chopped fresh thyme leaves
1	lemon juiced
1	tsp. chopped fresh thyme leaves
	Kosher salt
	Freshly-ground pepper
1	whole lemon (halved)
1	large bunch of fresh thyme
1	Spanish onion, quartered
1	head of garlic, halved sideways
1	quart of turkey stock

Directions

Place rack in the lowest position of the oven.

Preheat oven to 350 degrees F.

Melt the butter in a small saucepan. Add the lemon and 1 tsp. of the thyme leaves to the butter. Set aside.

Remove the turkey neck and giblets from the turkey. Rinse the turkey inside and out and pat dry with paper toweling. Place the turkey, breast side up, on a rack in the roasting pan and pour the turkey stock in the bottom of the roaster. Liberally salt and pepper the inside of the turkey cavity. Stuff the cavity with the bunch of thyme, halved lemon, quartered onion and the garlic. Brush the skin of the turkey with the butter mixture and sprinkle with salt and pepper. Tie the legs together with string and tuck the wing tips under the body of the turkey.

Position an aluminum foil tent over the turkey and place in the oven. Every 30 minutes baste the turkey with the juices from the bottom of the pan. If drippings evaporate, add stock to moisten them, about 1 cup at a time. Remove foil after 2 hours. Roast until a meat thermometer inserted in the meaty part of the thigh reads 165 degrees. Transfer the turkey to a large serving platter and let it rest for at least 20 minutes before carving. Serves 6-8.

Cornbread Dressing

Ingredients

- 2 tbsps. butter
- 1 small yellow onion, chopped
- ½ cup chopped celery
- 1 tsp. dried sage
- 1 tsp. poultry seasoning
- 2 eggs, beaten
- 1½ cups chicken broth
- ⅓ cup water
- ¼ cup unsalted butter
- Dry prepared cornbread mix, 16 ounces
- 2 (8 oz.) jars of oysters, drained with liquid reserved.
- Salt and pepper to taste

Directions

Preheat oven to 350 degrees F. Grease a 9x13-inch baking dish.

Melt butter in a small skillet over medium heat then cook and stir the celery and onion until tender, about 10 minutes. Stir in sage and poultry seasoning. Remove from heat.

In a large saucepan, mix chicken broth with water and bring to a simmer over medium heat. Stir in butter until melted. Lightly stir the cornbread stuffing mix into the broth mixture until the broth has absorbed. Mix in enough oyster liquid to moisten the dressing, about ½ cup or as desired. Gently stir in beaten eggs, then celery mixture and oysters. Salt and pepper the dressing to taste.

Place in greased dish and bake at 350 degrees for about 25 minutes.

Brussels Sprouts with Bacon

Ingredients

1½	lbs. Brussels sprouts
2	tbsps. extra virgin olive oil
	Kosher salt and freshly-ground black pepper
6	bacon slices cut into one-inch pieces

Directions

Preheat the oven to 400 degrees F.

Clean and trim Brussels sprouts, cutting any very large ones in half through to the core.

Place the Brussels sprouts in a large bowl and drizzle olive oil, tossing to evenly coat.

Pour the sprouts onto a large sheet pan lined with foil. Adjust so they are in a single layer. Sprinkle with salt and pepper. Scatter the bacon pieces over the sprouts.

Roast in the oven for 20-30 minutes, turning halfway through the cooking time until golden. Serve immediately. Serves 4-6.

Smashed Potatoes with Gravy

Ingredients

For Stock

1	whole head of garlic
2	tbsps. extra virgin olive oil
	Olive oil for drizzling
1	onion, unpeeled, quartered
1	leek, quartered
2	carrots, quartered
1	parsnip quartered
2	celery ribs, quartered
½	bay leave
½	tsp. black whole peppercorns
1½	cups dry white wine
⅓	cup soy sauce
6	cups cold water

For Potatoes

4	lbs. boiling potatoes
3	tbsps. unsalted butter, cut into pieces
3	tbsps. extra virgin olive oil

For Gravy

5	tbsps. unsalted butter
½	cup all-purpose flour

Directions

Preheat oven to 400 degrees F.

Separate 6 cloves from the garlic head. Do not peel. Drizzle with a little olive oil and double wrap tightly in tin foil. Roast until garlic is very soft, about 45 minutes.

While garlic roasts, heat oil (2 tbsps.), in a 4-5-quart heavy pot over medium heat until it shimmers, then cook vegetables, remaining garlic cloves (separated but not peeled), bay leaf, and peppercorns, stirring occasionally, until browned, about 8 minutes. Stir in wine and boil until most has evaporated. Add soy sauce and water and simmer uncovered, 30 minutes. Strain stock through a fine-mesh sieve into a large measuring cup. If you have more than 4 cups, boil to reduce; if less, add water.

Boil Potatoes

Cut potatoes into 2-inch pieces (peeled, if desired). Generously cover with cold water in a 5-quart saucepan and add 2 teaspoons of salt. Simmer uncovered until just tender, 12-15 minutes. Reserve ⅓ cup cooking liquid and stir butter and oil into it. Drain potatoes, then return to pan along with reserved liquid and coarsely mash. Season with salt and pepper and keep warm, covered.

Make Gravy

Mash roasted garlic to a purée. Melt butter in a heavy medium saucepan over medium heat. Stir in flour and garlic purée and cook, stirring 2 minutes. Slowly add stock whisking, and then simmer 3 minutes. Season the gravy with salt and pepper. Serves 8.

Creamed Onions

Ingredients

1	tbsp. unsalted butter
2	large yellow onions (about 1 lb.), cut into 1-inch dice
¾	tsp. chopped thyme
¾	tsp. chopped sage
¼	tsp. nutmeg, grated
¼	tsp. freshly-ground white pepper
¾	cup heavy cream
	Salt

Directions

Melt the butter in a large skillet. Add the onions and cook over low heat, stirring occasionally, until softened, about 30 minutes. Add the thyme, sage, nutmeg and white pepper and cook, stirring for 2 minutes. Add the cream and bring to a boil. Simmer over low heat, stirring occasionally until thickened, about 5 minutes. Season with salt, transfer to a bowl and serve.

The onions can be chopped and then refrigerated for up to 2 days. Reheat gently before starting to make the dish. Makes 6 servings.

Buttermilk Biscuits with Honey Butter

Ingredients

2	cups all-purpose flour
1	tbsp. baking powder
¼	tsp. baking soda
	Salt
5	tbsps. unsalted butter
2	tbsps. honey
1	cup cold buttermilk

For Honey Butter

3	tbsps. salted butter, melted
2	tbsps. honey

Directions

Preheat the oven to 435 degrees F and butter a large baking sheet.

Combine flour, baking powder, baking soda and a dash of salt in the bowl of an electric mixer. Mix on low to combine ingredients.

Pour in honey and mix for a few seconds. Pour cold buttermilk into the center of the mixture. Mix until just combined.

Transfer the dough onto a lightly floured surface and sprinkle with a little more flour on top. Knead dough 5-6 times and pat into a ½-inch-thick concentric circle.

Using a cookie cutter (about 2 to 2½ inches in diameter), cut biscuits from the dough. Rework dough scraps into a ball and shape it into a circle again. Cut out more biscuits.

Place biscuits on the baking sheet, leaving about an inch in between. In a small bowl, mix melted butter and honey. Using a pastry, brush each biscuit with the honey butter mixture.

Bake for 10-13 minutes until raised and golden brown. Remove the biscuit and brush with more honey-butter mixture. Makes 10-12 biscuits.

Christmas Cookies

Ingredients

- ¼ cup unsalted butter, softened
- 2 tbsps. granulated sugar
- 3 large eggs, divided
- 1¾ tsps. vanilla, divided
- ¾ cup all-purpose flour, plus additional 1½ tbsps.
- 1 cup packed light brown sugar
- ¼ tsp. baking powder
- ⅛ tsp. salt
- 1½ cups pecans or walnuts, chopped, toasted
- 1 cup flaked or shredded sweetened coconut, lightly toasted

Lemon Glaze

- 1¼ cups confectioners' sugar, sifted
- ¼ cup fresh lemon, orange, or lime juice
- 1 tsp. vanilla

Directions

Preheat oven to 350 degrees F. Grease a 9x9-inch baking pan lined with foil. Beat the butter, granulated sugar, 1 egg yolk, and ¼ tsp. of vanilla in medium bowl until well blended. Stir in ¾ cup of flour until well blended and smooth.

Press the dough evenly into the baking pan. Bake for 10 minutes. Meanwhile, beat 2 eggs, light brown sugar, 1½ tablespoon of flour, baking powder, salt, and 1½ tsps. of vanilla in a medium bowl until well combined. Stir in nuts and coconut.

Spread the mixture evenly over the hot baked crust. Bake until the top is firm and golden brown and a toothpick inserted in the center comes out slightly wet, 20-25 minutes. Set the pan on a rack. If desired, while the bars are still warm, spread evenly with lemon glaze.

Let stand until the bars are cool and the glaze is set.

For Lemon Glaze
Beat confectioners' sugar, juice, and vanilla together until smooth. Makes 12 bars.

Ginger Cookies

Ingredients

¾	cup butter, softened
¾	cup brown sugar, packed
⅔	cup molasses
1	large egg
3¼	cup all-purpose flour
1	tbsp. ground ginger
1	tsp. baking soda
1	tsp. ground cinnamon
½	tsp. ground cloves
½	tsp. kosher salt
¼	tsp. ground nutmeg
	Sugar cookie icing
	Sprinkles, for decorating

Directions

Using a hand mixer, beat butter, brown sugar, and molasses in a large bowl until fluffy, about two minutes. Add 2 eggs and beat until combined.

In a medium bowl, whisk flour, spices, baking soda, and salt until combined. With the mixer on low, gradually add dry ingredients to wet ingredients until dough just comes together.

Divide dough in half and create two discs. Wrap each in plastic wrap and chill until firm, about 2-3 hours.

Preheat oven to 350 degrees F and line two large baking sheets with parchment paper.

Place one disc of dough on a lightly floured surface and roll until ¼" thick.

Cut out gingerbread cookies into different shapes and transfer to baking sheets.

Bake until slightly puffed and set, 9-10 minutes, depending on the size of your cookie cutters. Let cool on baking sheets for 5 minutes before transferring to a cooling rack to cool completely. Repeat with remaining disc of dough. Decorate with icing and sprinkles as desired.

Sugar Cookie Icing

Ingredients
- 3 cups powdered sugar
- ¼ cup light corn syrup
- ¼ cup milk
- ¼ tsp. almond or vanilla extract

Directions
Stir together powdered sugar, corn syrup, milk and almond (or vanilla) extract.

Add milk, a teaspoon at a time, to thin, if necessary.

Baked Brie with Cranberry Chutney

Ingredients

1⅓	cups fresh cranberries
⅔	cup sugar
⅔	cup water
⅓	cup apple cider vinegar
⅓	cup dark raisins
2	tsps. brown sugar
¼	cup chopped pecans
¼	tsp. cinnamon
⅛	tsp. cloves
1	tsp. finely chopped ginger root
½	tsp. chopped garlic
1	round of Brie cheese
	Slivered almonds
	Cracker or French bread loaf cut in thin slices to serve.

Directions

Combine sugar and water in a heavy saucepan. Bring to a boil and stir. Add cranberries, vinegar, raisins, brown sugar, nuts, cinnamon, cloves, ginger and garlic. Reduce heat to low. Cook uncovered about 20 minutes, stirring frequently until thickened. Cool.

Heat oven to 350 degrees F. Lightly brush an ovenproof plate with vegetable oil. Place unpeeled cheese on center of the plate. Bake uncovered 5-10 minutes just to soften. Spoon ½ of chutney over cheese. Sprinkle with almonds. Serve with crackers or bread.

Spoon other half of chutney over, as needed. Refrigerate unused portion. Serves 8-10.

Lobster Bisque

Ingredients

3	tbsps. butter
½	cup chopped fresh mushrooms
2	tbsps. carrot, chopped
2	tbsps. celery, chopped
2	tbsps. onion, chopped
1	can (14.5 oz.) chicken broth
	Salt and pepper to taste
1½	cups half-and-half
½	cup dry white wine
½	pound cooked lobster meat

Directions

In a large saucepan over medium heat, melt the butter. Add the mushrooms, carrots, celery and onion. Cook and stir occasionally until tender, about 10 minutes.

Stir in the chicken broth, then season with salt and pepper. Bring to a boil and then simmer for about 10 minutes.

Pour the vegetable and broth mixture into the container of a blender or Cuisinart. Add ¼ cup of the lobster meat. Cover and process until smooth. Return to the saucepan and stir in the half-and-half, white wine, and remaining lobster meat. Cook over low heat stirring frequently until thickened, about 30 minutes.

Sole Almandine

Ingredients

- 1½ lbs. sole, orange roughly or other whitefish fillets, about ¾" thick
- 6 tbsps. butter, divided
- 2 tbsps. olive oil
-   All-purpose flour
- 1 large egg, lightly beaten
- ½ cup slivered almonds
- 2 tbsps. fresh lemon juice
- ¼ dry white wine
-   Lemon wedges
-   Parsley

Directions

Heat oil in a large skillet over medium heat then add 4 tablespoons of butter when oil is shimmering. Dip fillets in flour, then in egg. Place in skillet with melted butter and oil and cook until lightly browned and the fish flakes easily with a fork, about 2 minutes on each side. Transfer to a plate and keep warm.

Melt remaining butter in the same skillet. Add the almonds, lemon juice and wine. Heat through. Pour over fillets and garnish with parsley and lemon wedges.

Zucchini with Tomatoes

Ingredients

1	tbsp. extra virgin olive oil
1	tbsp. butter
1	tsp. minced garlic
3	medium zucchinis, cut into round slices
1	medium yellow onion, sliced
1	medium red tomato cut into thin wedges
½	tbsp. thyme
½	tbsp. oregano
	Salt and white pepper to taste

Directions

Heat olive oil in a skillet over medium heat. When oil is shimmering, add the butter. When melted, add minced garlic and cook for about a minute. Add zucchini and onion and cook until slightly tender and onion begins to turn translucent, about 5 minutes. Add tomatoes, thyme, oregano, salt and pepper. Serves 6.

Christmas Rice
(Easy dish my family has always enjoyed)

Ingredients

1	tbsp. butter
½	cup onion, finely chopped
½	cup medium green pepper, chopped
½	medium sweet red pepper, chopped
3	celery ribs, chopped
2	cups chicken broth
2	cups uncooked instant rice
	Salt and white pepper to taste

Directions

Melt butter in a small skillet. Sauté onion, peppers and celery over medium heat for 2 minutes or until crisp tender. Remove from heat. Set aside.

In a saucepan, bring broth to a full boil. Remove from the heat. Quickly stir rice into celery mixture. Season with salt and pepper. Cover and let stand for 6-7 minutes. Fluff with fork before serving. Serves 6.

Pecan Pie

Ingredients

1½	cups pecan halves or pieces
1	cup sugar
3	large eggs
¾	cup light dark or light brown corn syrup
2	tbsps. melted butter
2	tsps. vanilla extract
½	tsp. salt
1	unbaked pie crust or 1 (9" deep dish) frozen unbaked pie shell

Directions

Preheat oven to 350 degrees F.

Spread pecans in a single layer on a baking sheet. Bake for 8-10 minutes at 350 degrees until toasted.

Add granulated sugar and eggs to a large bowl. Whisk together until well combined. Add in corn syrup, melted butter, vanilla and salt. Stir in pecans and pour mixture into unbaked pie crust.

Bake for 55 minutes or until set. Shield the pie with tin foil after 20 minutes to prevent excessive browning. Serve warm or cold. Adding whipped cream is a nice addition to this traditional pie! Serves 8.

About the Authors

KATHY HAS WRITTEN THREE previous top-selling books: *Surviving Cissy: My Family Affair of Life in Hollywood*, *X Child Stars: Where are They Now* (with Fred Ascher) and *The Family Affair Cookbook* (with Geoffrey Marks). *Surviving Cissy* won the People's Choice Award at the prestigious Books by the Banks Festival and the Ella Dickey Literary Award. All books have received excellent reviews. Ms. Garver has written, produced and hosted 29 episodes of *Backstage with Barry and Kathy* for television as well as scripts for Family Tree recipes where she hosted home cooks who made their tried-and-true recipes handed down through the generations. Kathy also wrote and hosted *Star Watch*, a show about the celebrities on the Walk of Stars in Palm Springs, where she was also honored as one of the star recipients. Amid the four Audie Awards for outstanding work in audio book recording, Ms. Garver has also been honored with three Lifetime Achievement Awards (from the Young Artists Association, and two from the Southern California Motion Picture Council) and the Golden Halo Award.

SCOT HAS WRITTEN ONE cookbook called *Weaver Family Recipes*. He is a home chef and has been cooking for his family since he was about 8 years old. Scot has also written several screenplays. One was made into a short film called *The Outing*. He currently has two screenplays that are being developed, one a TV pilot and the other a feature-length film.

www.ingramcontent.com/pod-product-compliance
Lightning Source LLC
Chambersburg PA
CBHW062015220426
43662CB00010B/1342